Breaking Good

Don't play by the rules,

play to your strengths.

Simon Davie

Dedicated to Simon McGregor-MacDonald who helped enormously in the editing of this book, and who will be remembered forever for his strength in adversity.

ISBN:978-0-9924007-4-3

CONTENTS

PART 1

Breaking Good #1:

YOU DON'T NEED TO BE GOOD AT EVERYTHING: PLAY TO YOUR STRENGTHS

You were told you needed to be good at everything, and to fix your weaknesses. Now we know that great leaders aren't good at everything, they are outstanding in a few key areas.

Would you put Usain Bolt in the Olympic marathon to give him a development opportunity, or tell Pelé to be the goalkeeper for the World Cup Final? Managers in sport create a team based on playing to the strengths of the individuals within it. So why do managers insist on developing weaknesses that their staff have, in skills that don't matter? It kills passion and takes people away from what they're best at.

During times of change, especially when there is more to do, with less resource, we need people playing to their strengths not wasting time trying to be good at skills that they'll never need to use.

As a result of the Industrial Revolution's needs, maths, languages and science were the only things that mattered, and school reflected that. Now we also need creativity, diversity, empathy, curiosity and inclusivity.

The safe world is ending, where being good and working hard is enough to pay the mortgage. There are no safe jobs any more. There is, however, a new world emerging that is far more exciting and enjoyable. A world where you get to use the skills you are best at, and perform to your full potential in areas that matter most to you. Your industry is experiencing massive change, your job and organisation is not safe, so you need to play to your strengths to stay ahead.

This is the paradox of work in the new world: "the only way to be safe, is to avoid playing it safe".

PART 2

BEING GOOD ISN'T GOOD ENOUGH ANY MORE;
Looking for rules that need to be challenged.

At school you were taught that if you were good, did what you were told and worked hard, your education would get you a good job. Then at work, if you did what was expected and put in the hours, you'd be promoted, and a few would make it all the way to the top.

For the last 150 years that worked well.
But the rules have changed.

Now, successful organisations need people who know which rules to break to create value. There's a need for more focus on thinking differently, being creative, and leading. The trouble is school didn't teach you how to do that very well. In fact, you were taught the opposite; do what you're told and give me the right answer. If you had different ideas, it was best to keep them to yourself.

For what seems like forever, organisations needed compliant workers to deliver their plans, and the schools produced them. But the businesses of today need different skills. If your job can be broken down into a series of steps - and it probably can - then you can be replaced.

There is already someone willing to do your job for less money.

PART 3

WHAT NEXT?

What does the future look like in the new world?

There are so many opportunities that lie ahead for those that understand the shift, play to their strengths and know which rules to break.

BREAKING GOOD

Don't play by the rules,

play to your strengths.

PART 1

DON'T TRY TO BE GOOD AT EVERYTHING, PLAY TO YOUR STRENGTHS

Great leaders aren't good at everything

When we consider the great individual leaders, sports stars, surgeons and teachers they are outstanding in a few key areas - they don't excel at everything. Richard Branson is the first to admit that it's far more effective for him to spend his time thinking of ways to disrupt a complacent market than to work through the finer details of a financial report. He sticks to what he's best at and lets those with strengths in other areas look after the rest.

It's true of teams and organisations too. Manchester United has been one of the most successful teams of any kind in sporting history because it has some of the best players in the world. They wouldn't send their star striker to a 5-day goalkeeping training course, just because he isn't very good at using his hands. So we shouldn't insist on focusing all of our time on people's weaknesses.

Discussions about personal development plans with managers are too often focused on areas the individual is not strong at, rather than building up their strengths.

We are told from an early age to focus on what we are not good at, so it's hard for most of us to identify the things we do well, let alone develop them.

The Gallup organisation studied thousands of parents of school children and asked them the following question:

"Your child takes home the following report card from school, and it reads:

Maths A

English B

Geography B

Economics F

Where would you say you should spend most of your time?"

The vast majority of parents said they would focus most of their time and effort on Economics. It wasn't suggesting you should ignore all the other areas, but the natural tendency at school is to focus on weaknesses and let the strengths look after themselves.

Don't be good

In an insightful 2011 Harvard Business Review article 'Making Yourself Indispensable', Zenger, Folkman and Edinger analysed 250,000 feedback surveys from 30,000 leaders and found that raising just one leadership competency to an outstanding level can take your overall leadership effectiveness ranking from the bottom third to almost the top third of all leaders.

They also highlighted the benefits of standing out in at least one area. You're then more likely to succeed in a job interview than someone who is just 'good' across the board. If you have a couple of standout strengths in areas of value to the hiring manager, you will be even more likely to get noticed and progress to the next stage.

It's far better to have a couple of valuable competencies where you are a 9 or 10 out of 10 and a couple of 5/10 in non-important areas, rather than be a 7/10 in everything.

If you're looking for a new job or promotion, it's essential to know what you have to offer and be able to identify and communicate your strengths with clear examples that stand out from everyone else.

The Halo Effect

The great benefit of playing to our strengths is that there's a positive effect on the perception of the other skills we have. If you're amazing at public speaking for example, people are more likely to assume you are great at other aspects of your role too. There's no need to be great at everything, just make sure you're outstanding at something. This has been proven many times since Edward Thorndike first quoted the phenomenon in 1920. Since then, there have been halo effects shown in a number of areas from performance appraisals to jurors.

Professor Phil Rosenzweig from IMD pointed out that the Halo Effect even has an impact at an organisational level, and went as far as saying that "when a company is growing and profitable, we tend to infer that it has a brilliant strategy, a visionary CEO, motivated people, and a vibrant culture. When performance falters, we're quick to say the strategy was misguided, the CEO became arrogant, the people were complacent, and the culture stodgy".

If you have skills or experience that clearly add value you need to make sure people are aware of it. Market yourself well, so others see the value you add, which will increase your chances of getting a new job, promotion or pay rise – don't just wait to get noticed.

All types of business need to embrace this, to maintain competitive advantage, and meet the demand of customers that are expecting more for less. It's another reason why we need to develop a culture where people can play to their strengths, and stop trying to be good at everything.

That's not to say that if you're performing poorly at something that's critical to your job, that you shouldn't get better at it, of course you should. What's important is that you also focus on playing to your strengths.

Hire people stronger than you

It is now more important than ever to find out your strengths and focus on playing to them. It's in your boss' interest for you to play to your strengths too, but they're not necessarily going to find them out for you. Here's why:

Managers don't always want their staff to become great. It's a shame, but it can boil down to a failing on behalf of the leader. They fear that their staff will look better than they do, or even worse, take their job. It's easier if they have people around them that aren't better than them at anything, but easier is clearly not what we're after here.

Urs Hölzle created the team that built Google by hiring people better than him, saying "your greatest impact as an engineer comes from hiring someone better than you, because over the next year they double your productivity. *There's nothing else you can do to double your productivity, even if you're a genius.*"

It takes strength of leadership to have someone reporting to you that is more proficient than you at a skill, but that's exactly what is required to build the best team possible.

If you identify the top 3 core strengths of the four people in your team, you can have 12 outstanding skills across all the areas in which you need them to perform.

Compare this to the multi-national blue chip organisation that has 12 core leadership competencies and won't promote anyone until they are at a designated level across every competency, regardless of how important it is to their role.

The side effects are huge. People will spend their time

developing skills that aren't essential and never achieve greatness in their areas of strength. The ultimate result is you have an average leadership team, rather than a team that includes an outstanding innovator, an amazing public speaker, the best strategic influencer, and an analytical genius.

When asked what one thing Richard Branson puts his success down to "hiring people smarter than me". It is your job as a leader to help those around you be the best they can be.

If this means that they are stronger than you at certain aspects, then you're creating a team that's not limited by your abilities and has far greater potential.

Doing more with less

Playing to strengths is a powerful way to increase productivity, performance and morale. People love to do work that they are good at, and this way everyone wins.

All you need to do is open the doors, and give them the opportunity. If you need more from your staff because your business is growing, or if you have less people to do the same work as before, focus on their strengths.

In tough economic conditions you can't afford to ignore the strengths of your people, and if you can't hire more people, you need everyone performing at their best.

Shifting paradigms

The sun rises and sets every day. Except it doesn't.

Until 1616 when Galileo Galilei questioned the assumption that the earth was the centre of the universe, it seemed obvious to everyone at the time that the sun rose in the morning and travelled across the sky. He was ridiculed, and the evidence against him was enormous – how could we be speeding around the sun and not fall off?

Now it's as hard for us to imagine the sun rotating around the earth, as it was for them to imagine the earth orbiting the sun. Eventually people shifted their paradigms. When things have been one way for a long time, it can be hard to perceive an alternative.

Challenging the concept that we should focus primarily on our weaknesses is a paradigm worth reconsidering.

The education system is built to tell us what we are good and bad at, rather than teaching us to find out for ourselves. We are told repeatedly that the best way to improve our overall effectiveness is to focus on our weaknesses. It's one of the reasons we can be given 99 positive pieces of feedback and only think about the one negative comment.

We say it's human nature to focus on the negatives, there are even psychological tests that support this theory. According to Professor Nass (co-author of "The Man Who Lied to His Laptop: What Machines Teach Us About Human Relationships") the brain handles positive and negative information in different hemispheres. Negative emotions require more thinking and the information is processed more thoroughly. Professor Roy F. Baumeister has also researched this theory, and his experiments show that the level of upset someone feels at losing $50 is far greater than the level of happiness they'd feel if they found $50.

We therefore need to make sure that we identify the strengths of our staff, and then seek opportunities to play to them, as the natural tendency will be to focus on their weaknesses.

I'm not saying we should completely ignore negative points, but they are getting far too much airtime already.

It's time to change some simple paradigms, and the idea that our biggest development opportunity is to focus on our weaknesses, is one of them.

Imagine putting your life on the line to suggest something that is ridiculous to everyone else. Galileo was in this unenviable situation when he argued that scripture was wrong, and the earth was not the centre of the universe. Fortunately, you don't have to risk your life and face Galileo's fate of lifetime imprisonment to challenge your assumptions.

Standing out v Fitting In

It used to be safer not to get noticed, but there's far more security nowadays in standing out, rather than fitting in. The post Taylorism economy will pay for people that add value and you can do just that. The downside is that everything you've learnt about doing what you're told is not going to help you come up with new and better products or services.

We have been trained to follow rules where it's helpful, but now we need to shake it up and break a few things too.

Winners don't quit

Author Malcolm Gladwell has written extensively about the benefits of dedicating yourself to something rather than trying to be good at everything. In other words, pursue mastery of your chosen craft rather than fixing faults that may not be important.

Gladwell says that you need to work at a skill for 10,000 hours to master it, and backs it up with interesting examples of successful people in his book 'Outliers'. One of the highlights is his case study on The Beatles.

Before they were famous, The Beatles played 8 hour sessions, 7 days a week in small European pubs. Between late 1960 and early 1962 they performed 270 nights in just over 18 months.

By the time they'd enjoyed their first taste of success in 1964, they had already performed over 1,200 times. Most bands don't play that many gigs in their entire career.

Winners quit

Knowing what to quit and when, is the key. If you're working tirelessly on something that isn't working, stop it. Your skills are needed elsewhere, somewhere you really can make a difference. The trouble is most people are too proud to admit when it's time to quit, even to themselves.

Quitting, contrary to what most sports coaches will tell you, is not the easy option. It's often much easier, much safer, to keep investing more time and money into the project, job, customer, relationship, than to walk away at the right time.

So when is the right time? It's best to set the parameters of when to walk away at the outset, and then have the courage to follow through if that time comes. It's harder to know what conditions are right to stop doing something when you're in the moment, tired or panicked.

Persistence is one of the most important factors of success, but persisting in something that's not working is taking valuable resource away from a more critical area.

When I worked at Unilever I was involved in a major change of focus, to ensure that time and money wasn't being spread too thinly. In 18 months the company reduced the number of brands globally from 1800 to 400. It was a tough decision for the organisation to quit so many brands, but the right one.

Quitting is not the same as failing. Stopping the right

things allows us to focus our limited resources on what works, and delivers most value.

Know what success looks like and do everything you can to make that happen, even if it involves quitting some things along the way.
There's always a reason not to start, but I realised that you only need one good reason to begin. Fear will often give us cause not to start, but I can't say strongly enough how critical is the act of beginning. Once you have started, it creates its own energy and momentum and can provide enough intrinsic motivation to propel you forward in a way you never thought possible. However, it can be just as difficult to stop doing something, especially when you have invested a lot into it.

But don't quit because today's too hard, quitting to avoid short term pain is not valuable. Quitting things that are taking your focus away from a strength that's important can be the preferred option though. When you re-focus your strengths for the long term, you're more likely to become the best at what you do.

Trust your gut

We can have an instinctive ability to know instantly whether something is right or wrong, often built up over years of experience. As Malcolm Gladwell talks about in his insightful book 'Blink' this instinct is used by talented fire fighters every day, when having to make a split-second decision to get out of a burning building moments before it collapses. Some call it 'gut feel', others 'intuition', for some it is linked to faith, and for many it is something they 'just know'.

Your enteric nervous system, which plays a big part in controlling your gut, has its own network of neurons and neurotransmitters that are completely distinct from the brain in your head. It can think, remember and even learn; some even call it a 'second brain'. I'm not suggesting this is necessarily helping you make decisions, but perhaps the expression to 'go with your gut' is more apt than it appears.

We all have intuition, but sometimes we ignore it and don't recognise its use. The more we align what we do with our strengths, the better our intuition works.

It's helpful to listen to your gut, and support it, by making decisions that feel right, even if you can't necessarily articulate why. Successful leaders often have to make decisions without all the information in front of them. To avoid making a decision at a critical time, can be far more dangerous than going with what data you have available at the time.

I'm a big believer in analytical decision making, but if you don't have the luxury of time, or the additional budget or resource, it's ok to go with your gut. As with other decision making, it's just like a muscle and gets stronger the more you use it. It can also atrophy if you don't use it. Every time you ignore your gut feeling, you are less likely to listen to it in the future.

Put your mask on first

When your plane starts filling with smoke, losing altitude and is going to make an emergency landing, the message is crystal clear; fix your own oxygen mask first, then help others. If a parent ignores this request and follows their natural instinct to put their three children's masks on before their own, the chances are they will get 1 or 2 on before they pass out. Not only do they risk the health of their 3rd child, but they also now need help themselves. However, if they had put their own mask on first they could help all their children and then countless others on the plane.

The same applies to the leader who spends all of their time looking after their staff, or on their job in general, and doesn't look after their own well-being. Focus on looking after yourself, and you'll be far more use to your team and anyone else you work with.

There are plenty of narcissistic leaders that only look out for themselves, but if you're someone who's always looking after others, then sooner or later you'll burn out and be no use to anyone, even adding to the problem.

Don't wait until it's too late. Look after yourself, spend time on your strengths as well as those of your team, and the overall results will be better for everyone.

Choosing your work

One of Confucius' most famous quotes is "Choose a job you love and you'll never work a day in your life."

Being passionate about the work you do is so important. You spend most of your waking life at work, so choose something you enjoy.

It doesn't mean you necessarily have to leave your job, though you can change the role you have by focusing on the areas in which you have strengths.

"Love the job you choose, and you'll never work a day in your life", is also worth consideration.

To ensure you can enjoy what you choose you may need to identify what it is you really enjoy. When we're playing to our strengths we are happier because we're doing things that we are best at. When our strengths are in areas we value then the effect is even stronger.

Choosing a career path that is in conflict with your values will make it harder to be happy in the work you do. It follows that the higher you rise in a company with conflicting values, the more you have to suppress and the less happy you become in the long term. For example, if you're a designer that values integrity, but think the cartoon characters you're creating for burger ads are more about tricking kids than providing entertainment, no matter how hard you work, and what sales you generate, you will never feel truly happy with the work you do. In fact, the more successful the ads are, the worse you're likely to feel.

Working out what strengths you value is only half the battle. The other half is deciding how to bring them into the work you do.

One way to identify your values is to go through a list and circle those that resonate most with you. Here's a list of some values and attributes to get you started.
It can help to consider people you admire and think about what values they represent.

What is it about them that you respect? Are these important to you too?

Choose 5 words that are most important to you from this list:

Serenity	Peace	Impact
Meaning	Exhilaration	Dreaming
Friendship	Extroversion	Simplicity
Awe	Friendliness	Bravery
Restraint	Pleasure	Independence
Chastity	Entertain	Obedience
Privacy	Dexterity	Impartiality
Playfulness	Sanguine	Satisfaction
Leadership	Coolness	Sacrifice
Guidance	Introversion	Expressive
Experience	Belonging	Temperance
Meticulous	Challenge	Courtesy
Pleasantness	Involvement	Piety
Carefulness	Desire	Conviviality
Liberty	Dependable	Perfection
Hospitality	Harmony	Benevolence
Expediency	Drive	Devoutness
Lightness	Inspiration	Dominance
Worthiness	Credibility	Composure
Soundness	Thorough	Originality
Clear-minded	Mellowness	Calmness
Accuracy	Change	Inquisitive

Courage	Adventure	Intimacy
Candour	Imagination	Charity
Richness	Outdoors	Longevity
Competence	Insightful	Diligence
Intensity	Intuition	Realism
Ferocity	Depth	Status
Daring	Beauty	Discipline
Mysterious	Cunning	Audacity
Honesty	Relaxation	Respect
Sensitivity	Intuitiveness	Fairness
Exuberance	Aggressive	Hopefulness
Support	Reasonable	Service
Sagacity	Eagerness	Duty
Structure	Strength	Contribution
Rationality	Loyalty	Compassion
Speed	Stability	Acknowledge
Ambition	Resourceful	Kindness
Diversity	Discovery	Meekness
Accessibility	Advancement	Creativity
Assertiveness	Security	Effective
Majesty	Tranquility	Individuality
Buoyancy	Pride	Sharing
Selflessness	Generosity	Conscious
Anticipation	Outrageous	Partnership
Marriage	Cleverness	Self-reliance
Perkiness	Concentration	Reliability
Community	Learning	Resilience
Growth	Reputation	Optimism
Potency	Investing	Usefulness
Enjoyment	Amusement	Excellence
Recognition	Accomplished	Enthusiasm

Love	Articulacy	Adoration
Judicious	Pragmatism	Reverence
Dignity	Directness	Logic
Extravagance	Persuasiveness	Health
Sensuality	Gentility	Efficiency
Hygiene	Mindfulness	Dynamism
Holiness	Surprise	Intelligence
Devotion	Abundance	Shrewdness
Recreation	Passion	Energy
Victory	Stealth	Assurance
Mastery	Encourage	Adroitness
Wittiness	Availability	Sympathy
Appreciation	Heroism	Keenness
Justice	Control	Resolution
Reason	Affluence	Philanthropy
Rigour	Precision	Approval
Professionalism	Trust	Humility
Enigmatic	Capability	Ethics
Influence	Gallantry	Religious
Attentiveness	Prosperity	Self-respect
Intellect	Brilliance	Prudence
Modesty	Delight	Comfort
Thoughtful	Boldness	Care
Honour	Empathy	Affection
Nature	Elegance	Saintliness
Self-control	Charm	Success
Synergy	Country	Preparedness
Approachable	Frugality	Expertise
Continuity	Activeness	Agility
Artistry	Teamwork	Elation
Camaraderie	Competition	Proactivity

Solidarity	Craftiness	Motivation
Connection	Confidence	Alertness
Skillfulness	Ingenuity	Amazement
Punctuality	Poise	Refinement
Humour	Art	Curiosity
Closeness	Ecstasy	Fearlessness
Responsible	Nerve	Cheerful
Expectancy	Faith	Patience
Conformity	Polish	Conservation
Clarity	Intrepidness	Integrity
Organisation	Decorum	Cooperation
Science	Resolve	Commitment
Cleanliness	Frankness	Persevering
Zeal	Relief	Openness
Wealth	Discretion	Achievement
Sincerity	Power	Attractiveness
Tidiness	Rest	Altruism
Sacredness	Congruency	Decisive
Adaptability	Joy	Acceptance
Cordiality	Industry	Consistency
Direction	Bliss	Maturity
Endurance	Popularity	Completion
Openminded	Excitement	Exploration
Outlandish	Neatness	Contentment
Euphoria	Reflection	Inventiveness
Introspection	Economy	Certainty
Introspection	Correctness	Fun
Order	Helpfulness	Education
Niceness	Awareness	Balance

Are the words you chose in line with how you work?

If not, can you bring them in somehow?

For example, if creativity is something that's important to you, but your job doesn't easily offer you opportunities to be creative, you could first look at changing your paradigm, rather than thinking about changing your career, or even your job.

Find a way you can bring creativity, or whatever value is true for you, to the role yourself.

Even if you can't bring them in immediately, it can be worth being aware of, as at the very minimum you don't want your organisation to be in conflict with your values.

Playing to your Strengths

Step 1: Identify your strengths

Step 2: Highlight your most valuable strengths

Step 3: Find ways to use and develop those strengths

In order to focus on our strengths, you need to know what they are. This doesn't have to be a complicated process, but it's certainly worth investing the time to find out. Once you've identified your strengths, prioritise which are going to be most valuable to you and target ways you can showcase, use and develop those strengths.

Step 1: Identify your strengths

There are many ways of identifying your strengths, find one that works for you, or even try a combination of approaches.

Self Assessment

Spend some time looking back over what has worked well for you in the past.

- A situation that you were involved in that achieved a successful result.

- A time you received positive feedback from a manager, peer, stakeholder, friend or colleague. Perhaps it was part of your development plan, but it could have been something that you were involved in that went well, although not specified in your role.

- An occasion outside of work where you made a difference, improved a situation, contributed to making something happen.

- A situation that made you feel great afterwards, gave you goose bumps or simply left you feeling happy with what you achieved.

- Marcus Buckingham, an expert in Strengths Based Development from the Gallup Organisation says strengths can also be those qualities that give you inner strength, that you most enjoy or help you feel strong and powerful.

- Think back to school – what were you good at then? What did people say you had a talent for? What did you enjoy spending your time doing?

Just because this step seems like a simple process, it doesn't mean that it's easy. You may find it hard at first to identify your strengths, especially if you are not happy even admitting you have any valuable qualities. Try thinking of things you have done that have been praised, rewarded or highlighted, by yourself or others.

Find a place where you can spend some quality time thinking retrospectively. Where do you have your best ideas? It's unlikely it's at your desk, but it may be in the car, on the train, walking, running, taking a shower, making dinner.

Put some time aside and have a think of an occasion where you had a good result, or made a difference.

Behaviours

Once you've identified a successful situation - and if you haven't, there are other ways coming up - you need to highlight the related skills and behaviours you demonstrated, that you have a strength in.

The others

It may be helpful to ask others close to you what they think your strengths are. Choose people that know you well and have seen you in action. You may want to speak with work colleagues, friends, family who you can trust. Sometimes we can't see our own strengths as easily as we can see the qualities that others have.

Take a good look at yourself

The 360 Degree Feedback process supports businesses to help their staff identify strengths and weaknesses. A series of questions are given to peers, stakeholders, direct reports and managers, to provide feedback around two key areas:

- How do you perceive their performance?

- How important is it to their role?

By gaining insight from how others view our performance, we can see where we have strengths and even get the detail of how this differs between what direct reports see versus the manager. It can be an incredible eye opener and give us insights into our strengths that we otherwise wouldn't have known.

The process also includes a self-assessment of the same questions which on its own is a useful way of highlighting strengths at work, and used as a comparison with the feedback from the group can show how the difference between how others view our performance and how we view it ourselves.

Step 2: Highlight your most valuable strengths

Often underutilised in 360 degree feedback is the second area, **importance**. It's great to know where your strengths are, but it's even better to know which are valued most. If you have a strength that the organisation really benefits from, that's the one to focus on.

If you want to know what your strengths are at work, and those that are important, you can use the 'Clifton Strengths Tool'. It's also useful for helping your team find out where theirs are too.

By knowing the areas you are best at, especially those that are most valued by your organisation you can make the most of playing to your strengths.

If you have weaknesses, you can also determine whether they are in an area that is important to the success of your role and the organisation. If it isn't deemed critical to your role, it may well not be worth investing time and money. You would be better off increasing your efforts to become outstanding in a more valuable aspect of the work you do.

It can also be beneficial to gain insight into those that influence your role. You can also get your manager to provide their thoughts to provide a complete picture of your perceived strengths and those that are important in your role.

If you're looking for help identify your strengths in relation to your personal characteristics, there's another tool in the world of positive psychology. A not-for-profit organisation called the VIA Institute offers a test which will tell you what characteristics are most valuable for you. Visit **www.viame.org** to take the survey.

Step 3: Find ways to use and develop those strengths

Strengths Mastery

Once you've identified your strengths you need to utilise them. Become the go-to person in those areas. Find new ways to demonstrate your strengths to others so that they think of you whenever that need is called upon.

Look for projects which require the skills you have strengths in and make sure the decision-makers know about you. It can be as much about marketing your skills as using them, so make sure the key stakeholders know, not just your immediate team.

You'll become increasingly valuable the more people know about how useful your strengths are, and more likely to get noticed for all the right reasons. The Halo effect will mean that others are also likely to see you as more capable across your skill set, simply because you have demonstrated how competent you are in your key strength areas.

Free Education

If you want to increase your strengths, you may need to learn new skills. Historically, you've had to be picked by a University, but now this education is available to everyone with a computer and an internet connection. Daphne Koller, a professor at Stanford University has a mission to provide access to further education for everyone. Koller points out that until recently, university courses have only been able to cater for a few hundred people - those that can physically get to lectures and seminars. In South Africa at the end of 2012 there were only a few University positions made available, but still thousands queued up to secure a place. When the gates opened, there was a stampede which killed a mother who died trying to get her son an education.

Koller has a vision that everyone will have access to the best courses from the best instructors at the best universities for free. She co-founded Coursera that offered hundreds of courses from over 80 universities including Stanford and Princeton. The Machine Learning class has around 400 people enrolled in the typical 'in person' course. When it was offered to the public as part of the free online program, there were 100,000 sign-ups.

Massive open online courses (MOOC) are available all over the world and are giving opportunities to anyone that can access the internet. It's not only access that's improving as a result, there are tangible outcomes too. Each student completes assignments and gets a certificate at the end, which has proven to increase their chances of employment.

Changing the way we teach

In these online courses, every student has to answer questions to progress through the material which ensures they are learning. Imagine having 400 people in a standard lecture having to answer a question in each section before the lecturer could continue.

The MOOC approach is improving the impact of the lecturer, not reducing it as many had feared. Koller states "Lecturers at my university often complained that their students (in the original university format) didn't interact and the complaints were mutual. When they did ask a question, the vast majority were still writing down notes, and playing catch-up, and of those that were paying close attention and able to answer, the same few people would put their hand up to answer the question. So out of 400 students, only one person was able to answer the lecturer's question. This compares to 100,000 of the Coursera students who all have to answer the questions and learn, to progress through the course."

Steve Jobs famously dropped out of the university degree he was studying, only to return and 'drop in' to the lectures he was interested in. An opt-in approach to education will mean that you aren't restricted to the degrees offered by your local universities.
You can choose whichever courses interest you, and play to your strengths and passions.

Being chosen is no longer a barrier between you and further education - you don't have to wait to be picked by the university any more. Now you can choose any of the online courses and learn a valuable subject, or get a better education in an area you already have knowledge.

Achieving a degree from a quality university is still beneficial and in the current system will help you access more jobs, and although many MOOC courses provide a certificate to show you have completed the program, they are not worth institutional credit. So this adds another interesting dynamic to learning of the future, education without a direct reward. The idea of learning something at school and not getting a certificate or at least a grade is alien to a lot of students and teachers, but as we will see, it's playing a key role in the new landscape.

Does your boss value your strengths?

In 2007 one of the world's greatest violinists Josh Bell was asked by the Washington Post to play incognito in a metro station during rush-hour. With his $3.5m hand-crafted violin and fresh from his sell-out concert in Boston the night before, he played for 45 minutes. Very few people even stopped to appreciate the music, and he earned only $32.17 from 27 passers-by. It just goes to show that the talents of even the best in the world won't necessarily be appreciated, no matter how technically strong, if they are not valued by those around them.

It highlights the importance of making sure you market yourself well, and that you're in a place which values what you offer. As a manager it also highlights the need to be aware of your team. You may know how well each team member performs at the key tasks they are measured on in their role. But have you noticed if they have capabilities in other areas that maybe even stronger and could be utilised to the benefit of both the individual and your team?

What skills are essential to your team delivering?
Who in your team has strengths in those key areas?
What are you doing to support their development?

That's where you should be concentrating your training, not on things that they're weak in that aren't essential to their role.

What if my strength isn't something that I enjoy?

If your strength is in econometrics, but you've hated it for years, then you have to decide your priorities. Is your happiness more important than the salary they are offering? If so, it may be time for a re-think.

However, before you hand in your notice, spend time considering what strengths you have that your organisation does value?

- Can you find a use for your strength that will benefit the organisation and help them deliver their objectives?

- Is there a project you could join where they need your problem solving skills, diplomacy, or attention to detail?

- Can you reshape your current role to bring in your strengths and add value?

- Is there the opportunity to create a new role where you can use your strengths and help grow the business?

What if my strengths aren't valued by my organisation?

If your strengths aren't valuable to your current team, consider the above points in relation to finding an alternative opportunity in the organisation to use your skills.

If it's not valuable anywhere in the organisation, then take a look to see which other strengths you have that could add value to the area where you work.

If your strengths aren't valued where you work, and there isn't an opportunity to use them elsewhere, you could:

- Find an organisation that values your strengths

- Accept that your strengths may not be your income stream for now, and make time for them as a hobby.

Positive Psychology

At University I found Organisational Psychology the most fascinating and interesting aspects of my undergraduate degree. I was very fortunate to be mentored by Professor Cary Cooper, who was the best in the field of Organisational Psychology then, and many awards later including a CBE (one step away from a knighthood), is still a leading voice today.

The one thing that I didn't like however, was that psychology then was all about retrospective approaches and remedial tactics. Most of the content was about counselling and looking back into the past of people's experiences and how we could fix people by going back in time. Psychology was all about correction, and very little about future possibilities in which I was always most interested.

In recent years, positive psychology has emerged which uses psychology to help people lead happier, healthier and more productive lives.

Go with the flow

Mihály Csíkszentmihályi is a Hungarian professor and the world's leading researcher in positive psychology. He has taken strengths based development to new heights as one of the first psychologists to study what's right with people rather than what's wrong.

Csíkszentmihályi's work supports that when we play to our strengths we are more likely to achieve a state of 'flow'. He describes flow as the mental state you are in when you're completely absorbed in the work you're doing, and it feels like time disappears. Flow gives you a sense of energy and enjoyment. The more we get to play to our strengths, the more we are likely to master our crafts and become an expert in what we do.

One of his areas of study was looking at what makes people happy, and his research showed that contrary to popular belief, it wasn't money. Once you receive a certain level of income - it turns out, not much over minimum wage - your happiness does not increase in line with the income you receive. We are conditioned to believe that increased financial reward leads to increased happiness and even motivation, but neither are true.

Income has almost tripled in the last 50 years, adjusted for inflation, but the level of happiness has stayed the same. If you double your income, you are not twice as happy. You may have a friend that earns twice as much as you do, but they're just as likely to have the same level of happiness and even the same number of problems. This is because they too have a friend that earns twice as much as they do, who they look at in the same light as you look at them.

The system isn't going to point out this to you though, as there's a belief, even if it's unconscious, that this envy or need for more things, will keep you hungry and motivated to do more work for the organisation, so they get their results and don't have to find a replacement.
Nigel Marsh has one of the highest ranked Australian TED

video on YouTube called 'How to make work-life balance work' which makes the simple but insightful point that too many people "do jobs they hate, to enable them to buy things they don't need, to impress people they don't like".

Risk of Reward

There is also an assumption that financial reward leads to motivation. Business is decades behind the scientific research that proves this is not true over time.

Reward is a de-motivating tool in the long term and there is a much more effective and human way of motivation.

In his book 'Drive', Daniel H. Pink talks about motivation from a refreshing viewpoint, that I've been a strong advocate for since my early management days, and also as a parent. Supported by over 40 years of research he demonstrates that Taylorism's "reward & punishment" approach to motivating people like horses (i.e. wielding a nicer carrot in front of our noses, or getting a bigger stick to hit us with) is not effective for most situations.

Neither is the biological drive (hunger, thirst), going to be a suitable or practical motivator for most people over time.

Pink argues the third motivator called intrinsic motivation, enjoying the task itself, is a far more effective way of helping people become and stay motivated in what they are doing. It's based on research from the 1940s by a professor of psychology Harry F. Harlow.

He gave monkeys puzzles to solve and found those monkeys that got rewards for solving them took longer, and were less accurate, than those who weren't given any reward at all. They solved the puzzles just because it was an enjoyable thing to do.

We have this intrinsic motivation built into us, but school, parenting and scientific management can squeeze it out of us, replacing it with a short term focus on immediate reward. The business community at the time didn't like the results of the study, so it was largely ignored for 20 years until Edward Deci replicated the findings. He agreed that humans have "an inherent tendency to seek out novelty and challenges, to extend and exercise their capabilities, to explore, and to learn".

Pink provides many examples of how rewards result in reduced creativity, short-term thinking and reduced performance. My favourite is how he uses Karl Dunker's 'Candle Problem' to demonstrate how rewards by their very nature, narrow our focus and reduce creativity. You can try the puzzle out for yourself:

A group of people are given a candle, a box of tacks and a book of matches. To complete the challenge, participants have to attach the candle to the wall in a way that the wax does not drip on the floor.

Have a go yourself, stop here for a moment and try to figure it out before you read on.

The answer's on the next page.

The solution to the problem is first to fix the box that the tacks were in to the wall, using the tacks. Then put the candle in the box so the wax drips into the box, not onto the floor.

The trick is to be able to see the box as more than just a container for the tacks and see the multitude of other uses, including a candle holder.

To solve this problem requires creativity and divergent thinking, which are skills that are needed at work now more than ever before.

Even more interesting, perhaps than the solution itself, is what happened when the participants were split up into two groups. The first group was told they were being timed as part of research to gauge the typical time for the exercise. The other group was told they would be given a financial reward for completing the task.

Across all results, the incentivised group took 3.5 minutes longer than those who were just asked to complete the test without any reward.

As with the other examples in the book, it supported the research that showed rewards limit our ability to think creatively, and while useful for motivating routine tasks, are counter-productive for more complex processes. Our own internal motivation is more valuable than financial reward. It also continued to be an example of how turning work into play and doing what you enjoy increases motivation and performance.

Another example offered by Pink was a study commissioned by the US Federal Reserve, carried out by four world-renown economists. The experiment examined performance changes when various levels of financial reward were offered. The results showed that in 8 of the 9 tasks, increasing financial incentives led to worse performance. There was also evidence that showed it encouraged negative behaviours when individuals became so focused on large financial rewards.

Research showed that these types of behaviours could have contributed to major economic issues, including the GFC. Corporate culture and the attraction of massive financial reward allowed, and even encouraged, unethical behaviours within some prestigious financial institutions, that in the opinions of many experts brought the entire system close to collapse.

The reward & punishment concept works effectively for routine tasks required by the Industrial Revolution, and can work for those wanting to be the cheapest in the market. If you need someone to repeat a task over and over, in a highly controlled environment, then the best way can be to use the carrot and stick approach. However, if you want to win the race to the top and survive in today's economic landscape this isn't going to work. You can't use rewards alone to motivate people to innovate and come up with new products or better ways of doing things.

Today, jobs are complex and self-motivation is more critical than ever before. If you're expecting your boss to be responsible for motivating you, it is probably because you have been brought up that way.

The problem is that although it isn't your fault, the skills you need to motivate yourself out of the situation, are the same skills that would have avoided you getting into this place to begin with.

The good news is that it's not hard to get out of, but no-one's going to do it for you. You need to work out what you're best at, and what's important - then find ways to play to those strengths.

The Horse Power Misnomer

Ford's assembly line played a massive part in reducing and in many cases removing the need for horses for transport, and we are again at a crossroads where you may be at risk of being sent off to pasture, or worse.

We should also consider George Orwell's allegorical book, Animal Farm. Orwell uses animals to demonstrate many ideas, one of which is that leaders don't always have their followers' best interest at heart. Boxer the horse is the loyal and hardworking labourer who thinks problems can only be solved by working harder, and believes everything his tyrannical leader Napoleon tells him. Boxer also realises that once he is no longer useful to the system that employs him, he will be killed and replaced by another horse.

We are experiencing our own revolution as industries shift and we can't rely on being told what to do next, or just wait and see if help is coming. If you throw a frog into a boiling pot, it will jump straight out, but it you put it into a warm saucepan and bring it to the boil it will die. This is the effect of a gradual change, and if you're not aware of the current change in conditions, you'll only notice it when the shift has already taken place and the water reaches boiling point, but by then it's too late.

We all have the power to change, but it can require a paradigm shift from putting your hand up and waiting to be chosen, to taking control and picking yourself. Most importantly, it's the opportunity for you to do what you do best and put your strengths into action.

Hard drive

If you had a job at the Encyclopædia Britannica at the end of the 20th Century, you could be forgiven for thinking you had a secure job.

The barrier to entry was huge, Microsoft even gave it their best shot with 'Encarta' and despite their financial clout and market power, they could not take on the institution that had been around since 1768.

However, as we all know now, Wikipedia is now the most used encyclopaedia and has 18 billion page views every month. Over 20 million people have voluntarily contributed to its creation, and although 'only' about 300,000 have added content more than ten times, the top 5,000 editors have made over 180 million edits. That's an average of over 36,000 edits each; for no pay, no financial reward, no bonus, no car and no holiday.

So why do they do it?

According to their statistics, 63% of editors contribute because it's fun.

They are intrinsically motivated. It's believed that those that large contributors are professionals with well-paid jobs, but they contribute to Wikipedia because it gives them personal satisfaction.

It's not just encyclopaedias that are created and maintained free of charge. This open source community that, for no direct financial return, provides products and services for free that are well respected, and by no means small players in the markets in which they operate.

Consider Android, the operating system on hundreds of millions of smartphones. It is open source and the software can be distributed and modified freely by anyone who wants to. Firefox is an internet browser also used by millions of people that's open source, as is the Apache Server which became the first web server software to serve more than 100 million websites. Ioannis Stamelos, a professor of Informatics takes the view that the culture of open source can apply more generally within organisations, in contrast with more centralised models of development such as those typically used in commercial companies.

People work for open source for a variety of reasons, but the drive is more aligned with intrinsic motivation, rather than a financial reward. If you want your team to be more creative, productive and increase their performance, it would be a more positive start to help them identify and use their strengths in an area valuable to them, and your organisation.

According to Gallup only 17% of people get to play to their strengths at work. It may not be as easy as offering a financial incentive, but the opportunities are far greater if you help people master the skills that they are already good at.

Don't just manage, lead.

Hiroshi Yamauchi built Nintendo from a card-making company into a multi-billion dollar gaming giant but had no understanding of hardware. He didn't even play the games that made him Japan's richest. One of his strengths was in understanding what people wanted, user friendly entertainment.

While his competitors were investing in processing power, Yamauchi led from the front and focused his business on the playability of games. He was very proud that Pokemon, one of the greatest selling games of all time, was created for a console with 1% of the memory and 10% of the processing power of Sony's Playstation.

If you have a team, you can lead from the front. Think about communicating the context and the purpose of the task ahead, rather than just offering a dinner voucher for reward, after it's completed. Work together to create a vision for the team, help them see how their role makes a difference and contributes to the future you have mapped out. Ensure that they're able to play to their strengths, and then keep referring to the vision; don't just mention it once at the annual review.

You don't need permission

Seeking approval can be a cultural condition that requires someone else to tell you that you're worthy. You don't need permission, you can play to your strengths in your job today. Positive feedback and being told you're doing a good job is a useful reward, but so is seeing it for yourself. By all means, help others see it too, but don't look to others all the time for validation that you are doing a good job, that you are 'enough'.

A fear of not being enough is one of the leading causes of stress, and can lead to even worse problems. You don't need others to tell you whether you're enough, look at what you are doing and if you're getting the results you want, that's enough.

This intrinsic motivation is a much healthier drive than waiting for someone else to give you a reward.

Of course, you want your boss to be happy with your work, but you shouldn't give them total control of your future, that helps no-one in the long run.

Rebel without a symptom?

Health care can be as much about illness as it is about health. So much of health spend is focused on remedy, rather than prevention. Maybe it should be called sick-care, rather than healthcare. We live in a remedial society that often depends on a pill to fix the problem rather than focusing on avoiding the situation in the first place.

Workplace Training tends to have a remedial approach too. There are plenty of people to tell you what you're not very good at, and put you on a course to 'fix you'. How many times have you been told you need to develop a skill, go on a training course, then come back to work just doing what you did before? One of the reasons this happens, is because that particular skill isn't that important to your role, and you don't get the opportunity to implement the learnings.

Training companies are often happy to provide teaching on a topic for anyone, regardless of whether or not it's what the individual needs.

Rather than focusing on weaknesses that aren't in crucial aspects of your role, it's far more beneficial to concentrate on developing strengths in the priority competencies the role requires, and then mastering those.

Introverts don't need to be fixed.

Before the knee-jerk reaction of 'I need to fix you' is applied, consider whether there is a fix needed at all. Maybe it's a strength that you haven't noticed because of your own differing values and beliefs.

Introverts for example, can be overlooked when it comes to creativity, as Susan Cain, author of 'The Power of Introverts' found during her 7 years of research.

Cain points out that groups follow the opinions of the most dominant or charismatic person in the room, even though there's no correlation between being extrovert and having the best ideas. When it comes to creativity and leadership, organisations need introverts doing what they do best. If an employee prefers to learn on their own and they are happy to do so, then that should be encouraged. Forcing them to learn in a group setting constantly, is as unhelpful as asking an extrovert to sit quietly on their own all day.

Lexus, for example, thought that being an introvert was a problem that could be fixed with a ride in a car.

**"Introverted?
That can be changed."**

The response on social media was immediate and animated.

Being an introvert is not the same as being shy. For example, shy people avoid social encounters out of fear, whereas introverts just tend to prefer solitary over being social.

Microsoft founder Bill Gates provided useful insights into the importance of introverts:

"If you're clever you can learn to get the benefits of being an introvert, which might be being willing to go off for a few days and think about a tough problem. Read everything you can, push yourself very hard to think out on the edge of that area.

Then, if you come up with something, and you want to hire people, get them excited, build a company around that idea. You also better learn what extroverts do well, and hire some extroverts, like Steve Ballmer.

Tap into both sets of skills in order to have a company that thrives both in deep thinking, and going out into the world to sell those ideas."

Whether you are an extrovert, introvert or an ambivert (who has both), the key is to put yourself into an environment that's best for you and that values your strengths.

Cain says introverts can be passed over for promotion, so it's useful to ensure people that need to know you do a good job, know you do a good job.

Solitude is part of creativity for many people, it's not an

alternative to collaboration, and can be very useful.

As with the need for businesses to focus on these strengths, we all as individuals need to be aware of the strengths of those around us, especially when they differ from our own.

Contradiction paradox

Brainstorms rarely create an environment that brings out everyone's best ideas.

It's a flawed idea generation concept that has a bias towards extroverted people within a group, regardless of whether or not their ideas are more valuable than the quieter introverts taking part. Merely putting up 'No idea is a bad idea' on the whiteboard isn't enough. It does more harm than good as it gives the impression that everyone will be heard. Putting those words up is a contradiction paradox – the message itself is a bad idea.

Brainstorming is to creativity, what meetings are to efficiency. Once they had a use, but in today's environment, they can be as much of a problem as they are a solution. Yet organisations insist on investing time and money into them without really questioning their value, opportunity cost or sourcing an innovative alternative. But there are other options.

Shifting

A much better idea that creates opportunities for introverts and extroverts is a concept called 'shifting', discussed in Professor Amantha Imber's scientific and practical book 'The Creativity Formula'. Developed by Robert Epstein from Harvard University, the idea is an improvement on the typical brainstorming approach.

Instead of a large group pooling thoughts to generate suggestions and ideas for 20 minutes, Epstein has found a far more effective method:

1) Starting with a 5-minute session individuals come up with ideas on their own.
2) They then meet up as a group for 5 minutes to discuss and select the best ideas.
3) Afterwards, they work on their own again for 5 minutes
4) Then regroup together for the final 5 minute session.

It turns out that groups are better for selecting ideas, rather than creating them.

By coming up with ideas on our own and then bringing them to the group for selection, we are playing to the strengths of the individual as well as the team.

The shifting group will generate double the number of ideas of a group, and Epstein puts this down to the reduced exposure to disapproval. In a group situation we see people's responses, and even if they are told not to criticise ideas they don't agree with, they will still communicate their disapproval without even realising it, through non-verbal signals such as eye movement or body language.

Shifting is more fair, fun and focused; a great way to generate creativity and innovation.

The freedom to make mistakes

Albert Einstein once said that 'anyone who has never made a mistake has never tried anything new'. It's as relevant today as it was when he first uttered the words over 60 years ago. To enable a creative environment, it's crucial to be able to make mistakes without fear of retribution.

During the Industrial Revolution, a job on the assembly line required an exact response and result, and anything else would cause the process to fail and could even require the line or factory to be stopped due to a machine failure.

This definition of failure is what we still use today. But this is very different from trying something new, without a guaranteed response and not getting the outcome you expected. The word fail has itself failed. We still need a word to capture failure of neglect or not doing the right thing, such as when a CEO embezzles money entrusted to them and spends it on themselves.

Compare this to angel investors who put their hard-earned money into new projects intending to make serious money when the company is sold a few years down the track. They don't consider spending $1m on an investment that collapses as a failure. In fact, they see it as a success. I spoke with Stuart Fox who invests tens of millions of dollars every year, who told me that it's even more than that. There's a badge of honour for how much you've invested and lost, it shows how much of a risk taker you are; as long as you make it in the long run. They expect 8 out of 10 not to succeed, and then make serious money from the 2 that do.

Thomas Edison has been famously quoted saying he failed 10,000 times before finally inventing the first commercially practical incandescent light. When asked if he had got any results during his exhausting journey of discovery he replied "Results? If I find 10,000 ways something won't work. I am not discouraged, because every wrong attempt discarded is a step forward".

For years I thought that this was a feel-good story about how persistence pays off and we should never give up, but that's not the main point. To succeed and create the light bulb that went on to change the way we live and work, 'failing' along the way was in reality a core component to the framework of his eventual success.

Time for a new word?

We need to be able to define and describe this important part of such a critical process. If there is a failing, it is on the English language for not coming up with an alternative definition of the word fail that reflects the positive attributes.

Anthropologist Franz Boaz highlighted in his 1911 book 'Handbook of American Indian Languages' that Eskimos have hundreds of words for snow. For example, there's "aqilokoq" which is used for "softly falling snow" and "piegnartoq" which is only used for "the snow that can be driven on by a sled".

It's a matter of changing the language to change the perspective. There is a need to change our paradigm around failing, to consider a new meaning for failure and maybe even create an entirely new word for it. One for the act of trying something new that didn't work exactly, but was a step in the right direction.

When Shakespeare was born there were 250,000 words. Now there are 450,000, so if Shakespeare was alive today, he'd be semi-illiterate. We seem to be well equipped to introduce new words to recognise the increased depth of swearing, and even emojis are becoming part of the day to day way we communicate. So I'm sure there's room for a new word for fail when it applies to progress.

So how about we come up with a new word, to reclaim the art of trying new things that don't work.

I'd suggest the new verb could be:

newton (v) /'njuːt(ə)n/: to try something new that didn't work out as expected but resulted in a step closer to success.

Here's why:

1) It's derived from Sir Isaac Newton, who gave us theories and laws that changed the way we view the world today. Not so widely discussed, is that he wasn't always right. In 1679 he produced a theory that explains how planets revolve around the sun in an elliptical rotation. Nearly 300 years later, Albert Einstein came up an improved theory with extra accuracy that may not have disproved Newton completely, but certainly uncovered a lot of inaccuracies.

2) Another reason to choose the verb newton, is in relation to one of the world's most successful companies, that has had its share of failure. Apple developed the Newton and launched it in 1993. No-one knew what a PDA was then, or that they even needed a personal organising device. Even though personal organisers like the Psion Organiser had been around since 1984, Newton was the first product to use the term PDA. It was ground-breaking, but not an economic success, so after $100m and 5 years of persistence it was decided on 27 February 1998 that the Newton should be discontinued.

According to the current definition of failure, this product failed. It didn't re-invent personal computing, or make any money, let alone become the next big thing. But two of the Newton's developers then went on to create the operating system for the iPod. Many attribute the technical success of the iPad to the ground broken by Apple in the late 1980s and early 1990s, developing Newton.

Without the Newton there probably would have been no iPod, iPhone, and iPad. It may not have been a success in its own right, but it certainly contributed significantly to later phenomena.

Try using the verb newton for yourself. By consciously thinking about using a new word it will help you ask the question: 'Am I in an environment where I can innovate, try new things and create without fear of retribution, or are people fearful even to suggest a change?'

Use newton next time something doesn't go to plan, but you're a step closer to the goal.

Creating creativity

Enabling an environment where people can make mistakes, and learn from them, is one of the most essential ingredients of a creative culture. Mahatma Gandhi once said that freedom is not worth having if it does not include the freedom to make mistakes. Get newtoning - make mistakes, make lots of them, but make them for a reason that is to strengthen what you want to do better.

It takes strength to be able to create an environment where people can make mistakes without fear of repercussions but it's essential to do so, if you want to encourage creativity.

In 1830 Michael Faraday showed amazing sparks jumping between two spheres. If like me, you were transfixed the first time you generated your own source of static electricity, you can be forgiven for thinking that people were jumping up and down with excitement. Even in the presence of one of the most remarkable discoveries in history, they were unmoved. They asked him 'What's it for?' to which Faraday replied 'I don't know, what's the use of a newborn baby?'

They couldn't have imagined the dishwasher, vacuum cleaner or laptop in 1830, and it's equally hard to imagine life without them today.

We need to be aware of the possibility that something new may be valuable, even if we can't see why immediately. Critical appraisal can be helpful at the right time in the process. But there needs to be an idea generation phase first.

Risk culture

In today's world, we need to embrace change and add value, not shy away from it. In a challenging economy individuals and organisations are often scared to stand up or stand out, in case things go wrong and they get blamed.

The reality is that if you aren't creating a culture for your staff to try new things, and an environment where people can newton without fear of retribution, then you'll be left behind. We need to allow people to make changes and encourage risk taking - even if it's just in areas of low risk to begin with.
Do you create a culture where people can volunteer new ideas or challenge existing processes, without being worried that they'll be penalised for making suggestions?

Let them

If you've got the right people in the right jobs, they need to be given the freedom to make the decisions to get the job done, and support if the result doesn't go to plan.

It's far better to have decisive people that are using their role to execute the company strategy, even if they make an occasional mistake, than it is to have people that play it so safe that nothing changes.

If you have hired someone to do a job, then let them do it. If they have the strengths in the areas you are looking for, then back them, support them, and give them every opportunity to utilise those strengths.

Trust changes everything

Doug Conant transformed Campbell Soup through his focus on inspiring trust. As CEO and President, he turned around a toxic culture and the effect to business performance was immense. Conant made the point "before you have the moral authority to lead your team, you have to inspire trust. Trust is one thing that changes everything".

A shining example of how introverted leaders can inspire, Conant played to his strengths. He took a personal approach to his leadership and engaged his hundreds of leaders behind a vision in a way that others would have struggled. Every day he wrote 10-20 handwritten personal notes to recognise those employees that were performing well, which over his 10 years in the role totalled over 20,000 personal messages!

Campbell introduced a Gallup Employee Engagement Index which showed that for every 17 engaged employees, only one was disengaged. This exceeded Gallup's world-class benchmark of 12:1. For the 350 leaders, the ratio was an even more impressive 77:1

It also had a positive effect on company performance. From 2004-2010 Campbell's cumulative total shareholder return was 64%, nearly five times bigger than the 13% return of the market.

Strengths based development is not just about knowing what your strengths are, and those of your team, it's about creating an environment to enable those skills to flourish.

Creativity and diversity

It's easier to manage similar people, there's less conflict and people are more likely to get on with each other. That's great if you're setting up a peace process, but not what you need when you are looking to disrupt the norm and win the race to the top.

If you want a group to come up with imaginative solutions, then you need to be creative with who you select.

A range of different people with a variety of backgrounds, interests and viewpoints is going to give you a much better likelihood of coming up with something new, and valuable, than a group of like-minded people.

It may be harder to manage a team of people that have different views and opinions, but it's worth the effort. This applies to project teams too - if you want a creative culture, embrace diversity across the organisation.

Hiring managers often don't pick the best candidate, they choose people that are most like them. A study by Lauren Rivera from North-western University shows that hiring managers evaluate merit in their own image, and select people with an 'emotional spark of commonality'.

That's not to say that we should hire people that are a 'bad fit', but just because someone isn't the same as you doesn't mean they won't be valuable. If you want creativity, embrace diversity.

Managing in a change economy

It used to be enough for leaders to tell people what to do, and if you didn't do it, they'd ask you to do it again and again, in increasingly loud increments and threats. Fear is not sufficient to motivate people today, and fortunately many managers understand this, doing what they can to lead by inspiration rather than perspiration. The key to successful leadership is connecting with people, and whether it's staff or customers, we need to understand and relate to them.

Managers that still expect their staff to do what they're told, purely because they tell them to, are making life unnecessarily difficult for themselves. The key is to trust people to be who they are, not who we want them to be.

Bosses who don't bother to spend time with staff finding out who they really are, have to invest much more time coercing them to toe the line. This idiom comes from school where children were instructed to line up for a roll-call with their toes precisely on a line. It runs deep into the management style of those that expect their staff to do just that, literally or metaphorically.

It's a lot easier to invest the time in developing a mutual trust and it lasts longer too. Asking whether a team member had a good weekend can open up a conversation where you can both learn about each other, and is an obvious opportunity that is often missed. Of course, it takes more time in the short term but the benefits in the medium and long run are huge. During these conversations you learn about who they are, what motivates them, what they value and what benefits they offer.

It can be hard enough to identify our own strengths, let alone know what others' are, but having the knowledge that someone is not only able to analyse complex information, but that in their spare time they teach Mandarin, is worth knowing when the proposal from that new venture in China falls on your desk.

Maybe you'll find out that your kids go to the same school or that you both have a shared passion in string theory. Whatever you learn, it's going to strengthen the bond, and as long as you maintain a level of genuine interest, it will likely benefit everyone.

Breaking bad rules is good

Fear is a great way to stop people challenging the norm and finding out that there's a better way.

The good news is that if you have been trained to comply with a set of rules, you know the rules you need to break. Being a change-maker requires an understanding of what is needed and then knowing which rules to break to make it happen.

Clearly there are some rules which need to be followed, legal rules especially, but we are so used to living within fences we forget that there is a world outside.

Some organisations play to this fear exceptionally well. They create an environment where you're led to believe your company is the only place that looks after it's people and that if you went to work for 'the opposition' you'd be letting down your friends and colleagues. Not only that, you're led to believe that you'd hate the new place, the grass isn't greener, in fact there's very little grass there at all. All of this may indeed be true, but if we spend less time scaring people into working for us, and more time creating an environment that nurtures talent, creativity and most importantly trust, everyone wins.

Welcome to the Strengths Revolution!

Whether you work for a multinational, a small start-up or on your own, the time to embrace this change is now, and the window is not likely to be open for long.

You can bring your strengths to your current role, even if it means speaking with your manager first – it's in their interests too. If that's not possible, find out what other projects you can get involved in that will benefit from your strengths. Perhaps you can come up with a new approach to your current role that no-one else has thought of. Maybe it's time to look for a move within your company, create a new position just for you, or see what else is available that is more aligned with what you have to offer and enjoy doing.

If the fit isn't right for you, and staying isn't an option, it could be time for a change of company as well as a change in role. Find an organisation that is embracing the changes that lie ahead for them, one that will enable you to focus on your strengths.

Maybe it's even time to start something yourself? During the Industrial Revolution you had to have more than an idea to make an impact. You needed money and lots of it. Only a few had the capital to set-up a new factory and take their concept to market.
You also needed money for distribution and it wasn't long ago that only those with financial power could get their message across using expensive TV campaigns, celebrity endorsements and promotions. It took time to get everything built, products made and even longer to build up a following of customers to find out and decide to buy your product or service.

Now you can come up with an idea, source a manufacturer anywhere in the world, secure an instant loan, build a shop online and begin your marketing campaign.

It's possible to launch an innovative service or change the world today. That's not to say it's easy, but it's possible. You can, and must, connect with people and that is certainly easier than ever before.

If you have an idea you can make it happen; find out what your strengths are and get started.

You don't need permission.

You have everything you need to begin, to make something, or build something, help someone, change something, write a book, create an app, sculpt, sing, drive, kick, act, think, volunteer, analyse, break, start, stop, tell, help, craft, create, connect. You don't need a factory or a multi-million dollar marketing budget.

Whether you choose to make this happen in your current role or make a change – back yourself and start now.

No excuses

This new landscape also brings with it new challenges because you have less excuses than ever before. But you only need one reason to do something. There will always be excuses, but the exciting difference about today is that you have a window to make the most of your strengths. It won't be like this forever; you have to do something about it now.

There's a revolution taking place where the shift - from the system to the people - is happening for those that are willing to select themselves and take the leap of faith.

The world needs people now, people like you. You can make a difference if you want, you can lead – and you don't need permission.

PART 2

BEING GOOD ISN'T GOOD ENOUGH ANY MORE;
Looking for rules that need to be challenged.

The Shocking Effects of Compliance

As we saw earlier, from an early age we've been conditioned to do what authority tells us. As a child, doing what you were told could result in being rewarded for 'being good'. We were taught to obey rules without even thinking about it, and often without realising the effects. As an adult, it's not as beneficial.

Yale University psychologist Stanley Milgram ran an experiment that challenged participants to perform acts that conflicted with their morals, simply because they were instructed by an authority figure to do so.

The experiment required the participants to administer an electric shock to a stranger in a different room each time they got a question wrong.

They were instructed to continually increase the shock each time the stranger answered incorrectly, until the charge was so strong that it would be fatal. Despite knowing that the dose would kill the person answering the question, the participants still administered the fatal shock because they were told to do so by the authority figure.

In reality no person was being shocked, there was just a recording of someone screaming in pain being played at the point the participant gave the dose. The impact on the participant, however, was real.

This shocking experiment has been replicated many times by other psychologists, returning the same results. It indicates that people will act based on what they are told to do by an authority figure, even when it directly conflicts with their emotional and rational conscience. There is value in understanding the rules - and acting ethically and with integrity is of course important - but it doesn't mean you have to follow every rule. Knowing what the rules are is useful so we can assess which rules we need to break.

Costs of conformity

There are forms of compliance at work that we don't even notice. If the group agrees something is right, it's all too easy to go along with it. It's even more of a concern when we agree with something we don't think is right, or don't even notice.

In the 1950s Solomon Asch undertook an experiment where he asked a series of simple questions. These included showing a card with a single line on it, followed by a card with 3 lines, and asking which line it matched.

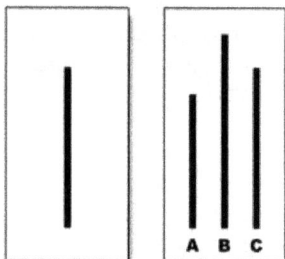

The questions were asked to the participant, and a group of others involved in the experiment, who were actors pretending to be legitimate participants.

The individual didn't know the actors were intentionally answering the questions incorrectly. The test was to see if the responses of the group impacted the actions of the participant. The results showed that despite the response being seemingly obvious, if the group gave an answer, most of the time the participant would give the same answer as the group.

If everyone is just going to go along with the general consensus at work, it's not conducive to an innovative environment.

For organisations to thrive in the new world, it needs people that can stand up for what they think is right, even if it is different from the crowd. Managers need to play a key role in creating a safe space where people can talk freely, and know that if they put an idea forward, they will be heard.

Blind Compliance

In another scientific test by G.R. Stephenson, five monkeys were placed into a large cage. Inside the cage was a ladder with a banana at the top. Every time a monkey went up the ladder the other monkeys were sprayed with cold water.

After a few attempts, the monkeys figured out what was happening and when one of them went up the ladder it would be attacked by the remaining monkeys, to avoid another soaking.

At this point, Stephenson substituted one of the monkeys, and the first thing that the new monkey did was to run up the ladder to get its hands on the banana. It was immediately set upon by the others and soon learnt that it was not a good idea to go up the ladder. A second monkey was then replaced, and exactly the same thing happened - this time with the first monkey replacement also getting stuck into the new monkey's beating.

Over the course of the day, the third and fourth monkeys were replaced and then at the end of the day, the 5th was taken out and substituted for another monkey.

What remained was a group of 5 monkeys, none of which had ever been soaked with cold water, but who all continued to attack any monkey that tried to climb up the ladder. They didn't know why, they just did it - blind compliance.

Compliance is the nemesis of creativity to the extent that sometimes we don't know who told us to do it, or even if we were told to do it at all. We are so conditioned from early life at school not to challenge the system, that we run the same reports, or schedule the same meetings, just because that's what 'we've always done around here'. Blind compliance is a rule that people followed to be 'good', but sometimes it needs to be broken.

How many procedures, processes, meetings, groups, products exist in your organisation that are there just because they were there yesterday?

To have a culture that embraces diversity, curiosity and creativity it's important to support people that come up with better ways of doing things. In a world where the only way to be safe, is not to play safe, there needs to be an opportunity for improvements to surface, be considered, and then if they're good enough, embraced.

What can you do to help shift this in your environment?

The rules have changed

Going to school, doing what the teachers told you to do, getting a job and working hard, used to be enough. It's not now.

For organisations to be successful in today's rapidly changing world, they don't just need you to do what you're told, they're expecting you to come up with better ways of working, offer insightful suggestions and create new ways of doing things.

Every industry is experiencing change, and to survive it needs people that are ready for the change, those who can provide growth rather than just follow orders. The trouble is that what they taught you at school used to help you get ahead - now it's holding you back.

A race you don't want to win

For many organisations, the pressure to be the cheapest has taken over from the need to be the best. Some call it 'the race to the bottom'. That race is one you don't want to win.

Here's an example; when a state government offers lower taxes to entice businesses to move into its state, it momentarily has an advantage. Soon after though, the other states are likely to lower their taxes to stay competitive. The end result is that each government has less revenue than before and unless the system is changed services will decline and people will suffer.

Historically, most companies made products and delivered services with the goal of being the cheapest, and for a long time this strategy worked extremely well. Now though, there is always someone that can do it at a more competitive rate.

Before the digital revolution, this wasn't much of an issue as your boss didn't know where those cheaper workers were. Even if they did, it was too expensive to bring them in, so overall it was not a viable cost saving exercise.

If you're a designer for example, this challenge is compounded by software that has made it simple for people to design things themselves. Gamechangers like Canva have made designing artwork, logos, posters, even t-shirts, really simple for almost anyone.

We still need amazing graphic designers, but the bar has

been raised. Now there's nowhere to hide for average designers, doing average work.

Until recently you'd have to order hundreds or even thousands of items too, whereas now the minimum order quantity is often just one unit.

Whether you are in design, tech support, writing stories, recording music, even making medical diagnoses, there's an alternative that means we all have to make sure we add value in the work we do.

With websites like Fiverr, you can get almost anything done by a freelancer, and it's likely to be cheaper. While this is threatening the jobs of in-house designers, writers, developers and heaps of other roles, it's also giving people the opportunity to get paid for something on the side.

Side-hustling

This rise of the side-hustle is also shifting the landscape. It used to be a novelty to have a second income from your own business. Nowadays, as I scroll through my LinkedIn feed or talk with Uni students, it can seem like the exceptions are those without a side hustle.

As long as it's not a conflict of interest with your day-job, and happens outside of working hours, it's something that can benefit the individuals and those organisations that pay close enough attention to how to play to their staff's strengths.

You can even make products yourself, when before you needed to own a factory. Alibaba.com is one of the world's biggest retailers and makes it easy to get almost anything you like produced and shipped to your doorstep.

Unfortunately for traditional businesses who've relied on being the cheapest, the problem is that strategy has been successful for so long that there's a reluctance to change.

The only way for most organisations to win today is to be different, to add value, to win the race to the top.

Is competing on price a viable position, when you'll never be the cheapest in the long run? To move your position away from price to one of value and benefit is not easy when profits are declining, and management is under increasing pressure to improve performance.

Don't wait, act now

There is a way forward, but you're not going to get there by waiting to be told what to do. You're probably going to need to break some of the outdated rules and play to your strengths.

The positive news is that the solution means you'll enjoy your job more than ever before, and probably be even more successful.

So how did we get here? Let's go back to the start of the Industrial Revolution.

The Industrial 'Revelation'

It's easy to think that the education system has been around forever, but until 150 years ago, only those with money were formally educated.

In the late 1800s the Industrial Revolution was in full swing, production wasn't able to keep up with demand, and insufficient labour was a key problem. In a radical moment of its time, it was proposed that people who weren't considered elite would be allowed to be educated, if given the necessary support and tools.

A decision was made to provide free education to children between 5 and 12 years old. This revelation resulted in the supply of workers needed to fill the factories and increase productivity, and was the basis for a revolution that would change the industrial world forever. This seismic shift created a massive resistance from taxpayers, who didn't think they should be paying for the poorest people in the country to go to school.

The cultural focus on science was gaining momentum as an alternative to traditional faith-based and religious ideals. The 'Age of Enlightenment' had created a movement of people that saw science as an alternative way of life to religion, which had been providing the answers to most questions until this time. In 1870 the school system was set up to teach the skills most valuable to the economy; maths, science and languages. Teachers ensured discipline, the students did what they were told, and left school knowing that they would be given a job.

It worked well, schools were producing 'factory ready' individuals who were able to perform all the tasks needed by the industrial revolution that was changing the world.

A Ford Classic

The creation of the education system coincided with the breakthrough of Frederick W. Taylor, an American mechanical engineer. Taylor was making his mark during the Industrial Revolution as the world's first management consultant with his concept of scientific management. His theory begun its development in the early 1880s and went on to shape industry for the next 100 years.

In December 1913 Henry Ford built from Taylor's theories to create his first assembly line to make his now famous, Model T car. By driving down costs, using an assembly line where people did the same task over and over again, he was able to make cars that more people could afford.

Workers were instructed to carry out very specific tasks, and production became increasingly efficient. This lowered costs drastically and made the cars affordable to the masses, which drove demand and in turn demanded more workers to supply more cars.

One of Ford's key strengths was how he treated his workers. In 1914 he decided to pay them more than double their salary, raising their daily pay to $5. The next day over 10,000 people applied to work at his factory.

Economic conditions were harsh, so it wasn't surprising that the company was in such demand. However, this was more than paying top wages, Ford also reduced the working day to 8 hours and linked their wages directly to productivity.

Reducing hours, increasing productivity

Rather than just being paid to turn up, people were given more money if their productivity increased. It was a moment that changed the industrial world.

So did his decision in 1926, with his son Edsel Ford, to introduce the 5-day week, stating that "to live properly, workers needed more time to spend with their family".

Very quickly, Ford workers realised how lucky they were, and with thousands of people almost literally waiting at the door to take their jobs, a sense of loyalty was soon established. Each worker had a very clearly defined job on the assembly line. They would undertake their task hundreds of times each day knowing that as long as they continued to do so, all would be well.

So the stage was set with happy, well-paid workers who had work-life balance.

Ford realised there were better ways of manufacturing and became very rich, and importantly so did the workers. Life for many improved dramatically, and if you weren't one of Ford's employees, you wanted to be.

Not only did he create a profitable market and improve the lives of the thousands of workers in his employ, he revolutionised transport which had far-reaching impacts, that he could never have imagined at the time.

Fear Factory

For thousands of years the skills of crafts such as carpentry had given those with talent an income. Suddenly, people had traded their skills, crafts, strengths and passions for the opportunity to get paid high wages and the stability of a long term job that almost anyone could do.

Yet what was seen to be a very happy workplace, was full of fearful employees. It was evident that if they did what they were told to do, they would be rewarded with a great life. But if they didn't conform, the alternative was only too obvious; they were easily replaceable.

School Rules

The school system was designed and created to produce workers that fitted the factory model. If you did what you were told at school and worked hard, you'd succeed.

As long as you continued to play by the school rules you would be practically guaranteed a stable job by the time you left school.

Thanks to Fordism there were also management opportunities to earn even more money, for those that were given grades at the top of their class.

The Office Works

When offices started to become popular, they behaved exactly like factories. People were told what to do by their boss and rewarded with a safe job, paid time off for holidays and some were given bonuses. Just like in factories, if the workers did as instructed, stayed loyal to the company, and connected with the right people, they would be offered a promotion with more money and status. It was great news for everyone. Workers and bosses got a safe job, and the owners made a fortune. As with the factories of the early 1900s, offices were able to become increasingly productive and reduce costs for the company through efficiencies. Also, like Ford's workers, most were very appreciative of the safety and security that their income provided them.

So offices, factories and government systems were created thanks to a foundation of compliance and a regular income.

With the increase in people getting mortgages, there was another reason for workers to stay at work. Employers picked up on this, which gave them more control of their staff, as the mortgages created a Sword of Damocles above their heads. For so many years this worked very well for the nations that adopted this approach - but now the rules have changed.

Post Fordism

For the last 150 years we needed compliant workers that understood the academic subjects, so we made it compulsory for everyone to be taught them. We then filled any gaps in the timetable with the humanities such as geography, social studies, history and if there was room we'd squeeze some art in there too.

Today's education system is still heavily biased towards academic subjects like maths, languages, sciences and engineering, but with an economy that increasingly demands creativity, innovation and identifying opportunities, we need a new approach.

The race to the top

You don't win the race to the top by keeping your ideas to yourself in meetings, and by accepting the status quo. We were conditioned to think that the best way to stay safe, was to get a secure job and work hard.

In the 1980s Mike Stewart was an inspirational leader in shopper analysis for leading blue chip companies. He very rarely did what he was told, which didn't always go down well with his business partners, but his reputation for coming up with new and exciting ideas for clients was second to none. He continually challenged the norms and was polarising in his approach, and those that were courageous enough to take his ideas on board, did very well from it. Acknowledged as the brain behind some of the most significant shifts in how retailers viewed their customers, Mike influenced the decisions of some of the largest retailers when they changed their store layout to focus on customer needs. This was in stark contrast to segmenting products based on the manufacturing-centric approach used for decades. For example, by placing tomato dips next to corn chips instead of next to tomato sauces, sales increased dramatically. It's taken for granted now, but he was a revolutionary for his time.

These days the messages coming from retailers are nearly always price related. If you ask a manufacturer now, they'll probably tell you that although the retailers are asking for the next big idea, what they want is the lowest price they can get. The only option for manufacturers is to do what the retailer tells them, or face being replaced by a cheaper alternative. So some of the smartest brains in the game have their amazing ideas ignored in favour of lower prices and reduced margins.

Customer expectations are also much higher now, which compounds the need for manufacturers to develop a strength in creativity. Ten years ago, if you bought the cheapest brand you would be purchasing a far inferior product than the mainstream and premium brands. Low-priced baked beans had a higher water content than their premium competitors, and you needed five times the amount of dishwashing liquid if you bought the cheap brands. Now, there's less difference, and you'll rarely find a product that is so bad you can't use it. If you do, the store will probably give you a refund. It's the same with hair-driers, cars and roof tiles – you can buy the cheapest in the shop and it will work, and if it doesn't, you can get your money back.

There is now virtually no risk for the customer to buy the cheapest product any more. The risk lies squarely with those that bring it to market.

The School Factory

The education system was built to support the Industrial Revolution, and it's modelled on the image of factories too.

As one of the most respected voices in education, Sir Ken Robinson points out: "schools are organised along a factory model with ringing bells to communicate start and finish times, divided into separate subjects, and children educated in 'batches' split by age as if somehow their date of manufacture is the most important aspect of who the child is".

You're not wrong

Robinson also observes that one of the skills that is so valuable to today's organisations is divergent thinking; to be able to think of lots of possible answers to a question. The traditional academic route at school, however, often teaches us that there is only one correct answer and that's the one in the teacher's edition. In a system driven by standardised testing, there's little room for more than one solution, and we all pay the price.

We're encouraged to believe that knowledge is the most critical determinant as to whether someone will be successful. But in a world where most information can be found through a quick online search, this is becoming increasingly less important. As Susanne Langer, an American mind and art philosopher pointed out, what's far more important to knowing an answer is being able to ask the best questions.

Academic intelligence is also not a measure across everything important. It's primarily a measure based on a model for deductive reasoning, factual knowledge and memory. It creates a clear divide between people that are 'academic' and those that are 'non-academic', which has led to a lot of brilliant people thinking they're not.

What about communication, problem-solving, creativity and collaboration? The issue isn't just that there is not enough focus on these areas, the problem is that school system can kill these skills off:

You were a creative genius

George Land and Beth Jarman studied 1,600 children aged 3-5 in eight tests for divergent thinking. The same tests were used by NASA to select innovative engineers and scientists.

Remarkably 98% of the children scored at the genius level. They then tested them 5 years later and these results showed only 30% scored at the highest level.

After another 5 years they were tested again, and as 13-15 year-olds it had fallen to only 12% of children scoring top marks for creativity.

Worryingly, in tests of 280,000 adults aged 25 years and over, just 2% were at the genius score.

Why is it that 98% of children start as a creative genius and by the time they left school nearly all had lost it?

Small children view the world with a very open, and innocent mind, and live in a world where anything is possible. Once they start school there are rules to follow, and they can be told that their answer is wrong, simply because it's not what the teacher was expecting.

Robinson has extensively researched creativity in children. He suggests that if your friend tells you that they can't swim, it's unlikely that you'd assume they have some genetic problem that prohibits them from ever being able to navigate the length of a swimming pool. You probably think that they just haven't been taught how to swim yet.

It should be the same with creativity. It isn't something that is reserved for people in turtle neck jumpers or quirky T-shirts. If you're not creative it's because you've forgotten how, and the good news is that you can learn to be again.

'It's easier to build strong children than fix broken adults' Frederick Douglass

I can remember very clearly one of the first instances my innocence was taken down a peg, and I realised that my definition of creative writing wasn't the same as my English teacher. He asked the Grade 2 class to write a creative story with the title 'A storm in a teacup'. I loved writing so I got straight into it, and began my story, which met the brief and gave me a lot of pleasure creating. I was very keen to get the teacher's approval, but unfortunately he didn't appreciate it at all. His level of distaste for my work was only surpassed by my Mum's level of anger at his remarks. It transpired that he had not appreciated my interpretation of a storm in a teacup. My colourful story about the perfect storm taking place inside a teacup fell well short of his expectations. Even after a heated Parent/Teacher discussion, he still refused to budge, and allow for creativity. It's experiences like these that stop children from letting their imagination run, and the conditioning process begins, to be someone else that has to 'fit in'.

School Uniform, Uniform School

Uniformity is actively encouraged at school in a variety of literal ways such as uniforms, school rules, and less obvious ways like awards for being quiet in assembly. We also teach children to put their hand up and wait to be chosen, rather than picking yourself, which is much more relevant in today's world of work, where those sit quietly and wait get left behind.

A sense of approval can be what we're looking for so we can meet our fundamental need to belong. Whether it's our parents, siblings, teachers, friends or a cuddly character selling hamburgers on TV, the need to fit in gets more entrenched as we get older. There are incentives from day one, such as awards at school for sitting still in class, even though this is not a natural state for a child to be in, or the best way for every child to learn and process information.

It continues with equally clear disincentives for going against the system, in the form of detentions, or humiliation in front of the class or school.

Conformity and uniformity play a structural role in our formative years, as a result of the system set up to create compliant workers. Yes, we need children to show respect at school, and there are of course many situations where they need to do what they're told, but it shouldn't be at the expense of developing creative individuals, we need them too.

It's not cheating; it's collaborating

Collaboration is an essential skill, but at school it can be discouraged, to deter cheating. There are stringent measures to stop children working with other students to get to the answer that the teacher is looking for. Copying the answer is not ok, but there are occasions when working together to find a solution is beneficial. The message against using someone else's idea, even if it's to complement your own can be loud and clear; don't cheat. Yet in business, if you're not able to collaborate and communicate with colleagues, or to take someone's idea and add value to it, you have limited worth.

It's not cheating if you take an idea that worked somewhere else, and apply it to your problem. It's a very valuable skill. I'm not suggesting people should plagiarise or steal patents, but we need to be less concerned with whether an idea is entirely original, and focus more on how we use information, bring together different concepts and apply these insights to solve problems.

Thomas Edison put it best; "Ideas have to be original only with regard to their adaptation to the problem at hand".

The Standardisation Standard

Standardised tests were originally designed to make it easy to gauge how well a student was performing, and identify who would be best placed for management roles in the factories.

Now standardised testing is a multi-billion dollar industry, used to judge schools and teachers, and impact school funding levels.

The tests have too much academic focus for today's world and need more balance for subjects such as humanities and the arts. They have become a toxic tool for bureaucratic system managers, and in the narrow areas in which they are applied they are ineffective and dangerous.

People are being educated to be like machines with binary responses; answers are either right or wrong. When you are testing large volumes of students, it works out well that maths, languages and science are not subjective. It's great for those that can retain facts and demonstrate powers of deductive reasoning so they can get to a conclusion based only on known facts. There is no room for ambiguity or subjectivity, so it's easy to test people this way.

It was ideal for the factory's needs too, and ensured that people with the ability to remember and follow instruction would be identified. This approach to education also made it possible to replace people easily. If they didn't comply, or if they weren't able to work, it was simple to bring in someone with identical skills.

From an industrial perspective this was perfect, as you had a constant supply of workers, and you were able to guarantee continued production and keep wage costs low.

Divergent and Convergent Thinking

Convergent thinking is based on using facts to come up with the 'right' answer to a problem, and is closely aligned to the way we assess academic subjects.

Divergent thinking enables individuals to come up with new ideas and possibilities which are essential in winning the race to the top. This type of thinking is more likely to be associated with the arts and humanities.

This way of analysing thinking was identified in a 1967 publication called 'Contrary Imaginations' by British psychologist Liam Hudson. He studied English school children and discovered that intelligence did not accurately measure ability for everyone and identified the two types of thinking.

Its consistency of solution lends convergent thinking to standardisation and grading, with which we have become increasingly obsessed over the last 50 years. It has become so easy to test and grade, that it has heightened the focus on convergent thinking.

There is still a need for convergent thinkers, but we must also pay closer attention to divergent thinking, and come up with better ways for its testing - the future depends on it.

Have you backed up?

Rather than help children play to their strengths, we've created a sense of fear for anyone that wants to focus on subjects outside of the socially acceptable academic fields. That fear is not with us from birth, we instil it into our children.

If you have ever tried to focus on the humanities or arts whether it was geography, physical education, acting, painting, or music, it is very likely that you were told that you needed a back-up. Choose anything other than academic subjects, and from day one you're probably already getting the message that you'll likely fail. Creating fear is what the system does incredibly well. If you don't do what you are told, you are likely to be ostracised and ridiculed for your differences. However, we should be taught to celebrate differences not be scared of them.

Diversity is so important when it comes to developing new ideas. It's not very useful on the floor of an assembly line, but it's extremely valuable when problem solving or being creative.

Strength in Diversity

We need to encourage diversity and inclusion from an early age, so that we don't repeat the issues that the current adult generations are facing. Diversity isn't just about making things fair; although that is extremely important too. We need variety to create effective business teams, problem solvers and teams that can understand and relate to an increasingly diverse customer base.

In November 2006, YouTube was acquired by Google and had some of the smartest minds in the world on the development team. One of the first jobs they had was to create a mobile app for users to upload their videos.

The trouble was that these world-class coders couldn't work out why 10% of the videos were being uploaded upside down. They worked long hours, brought in developers from other teams, and still couldn't understand what was causing the bug.

It wasn't until a left-handed programmer happened to be added to the team, that they were able to replicate the issue, and determine what was causing the problem. People using their left hand to record videos, typically held their phone the other way up to right-handed users. It was that simple, and was fixed immediately. They hadn't been able to identify the issue until then, as all the people on the team had been right-handed.

This problem runs deeper, now we are living in an increasingly AI driven world, where code runs so much of our lives. Without diversity in software development teams for example, we're going to get software with a bias towards white, straight, cis-gendered males. In a world where coding is now built into so much of what we do, this impacts us all as a society. Examples like the automatic hand-soap dispenser that only worked when a white person's hand was put underneath, shows how horrifically discriminatory things are. Just because it wasn't intentional discrimination - it was the unconscious bias of the white product team - the impact is the same, and it's not good enough.

Programed Inequality

According to a PwC study, 75% of the fastest growing jobs require significant training in science and maths. The trouble is that only 18% of Australian graduates are coming from STEM disciplines (Science, Technology, Engineering and Maths), and it's the same case in many other countries. Of the already low number of people graduating from those STEM degrees, even more concerning, is only 16% are women.

Engineering and Tech companies are often male dominated, but it hasn't always been this way. Historically, being a 'computer'- someone who computes - was seen as a menial task, and was a job mostly undertaken by women. In the post-war era though, it became an increasingly important. As technology historian Marie Hicks wrote about in her book "Programmed Inequality" there was concern that women would leave the workforce when they got married, so governments focused heavily on creating a male dominated workforce.

What Happened To Women In Computer Science?

% Of Women Majors, By Field

■ Medical School   ■ Law School   ■ Physical Sciences   ■ Computer science

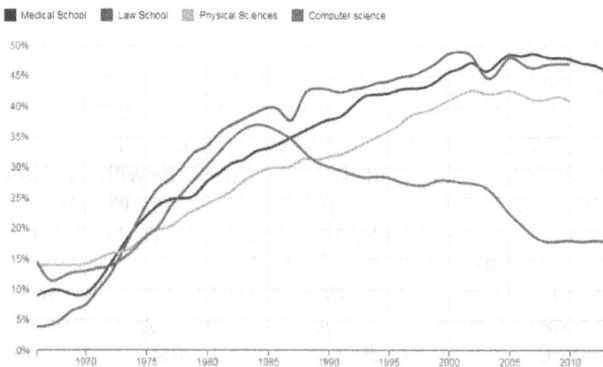

Source: National Science Foundation, American Bar Association, American Association of Medical Colleges
Credit: Quoctrung Bui/NPR

In the 1970s women started to return to areas such as Computer Science. But in the mid 1980s, around the time that home computer games were taking off, and marketed primarily to boys, there was a steep decline to the levels we have today.

Low numbers of women in STEM is not a women's problem. It's a societal issue.

STEM related roles tend to be paid better on average too, so from a gender pay gap perspective, if there were more women in STEM roles, the gender pay gap could be reduced.

However, with 75% of the fastest growing jobs requiring STEM skills, and women statistically less likely to secure these roles, the gap is going to keep widening until we fix the system.

If we don't address this issue it's more than possible that we won't have enough people to create and fill the STEM roles of the future. If we do, there will be more roles for all genders.

Bias behind the Screen

Consider the now famous example of gender bias in orchestra recruitment. Until the 1970s over 95% of orchestra members were male. Apparently, there was a certain musical sound that was needed and females couldn't manage it. The gender bias in auditions was ignored, and men kept hiring men, citing the special sound that was being sought after.

So the recruiters bluff was called, and auditions begun taking place behind a screen so they couldn't see the musicians as they played.

Unsurprisingly, the numbers of successful female candidates increased significantly. The system wasn't perfect though, as the sound of high heels walking onto the stage also influenced decisions during the auditions. Once everyone was asked to remove their footwear, the process improved again.

Typically, orchestras, now have 40% female members. There's still a way to go, but the proof is there that systems can be made fairer, with simple procedural changes.

Résumé Bias

In an experiment by Hays called "Gender Diversity: Why aren't we getting it right?", over 1000 hiring managers were asked to review a resume. Half got a resume from "Simon Cook", the other half got an identical resume but from "Susan Campbell".

The results were stark in contrast: Managers put forward the male candidate 27% more often than the female candidate with an identical resume.

This means that for every 100 identical candidates selected for interviewing from resumes, 44 would be female, and 56 male.
In other words, women need to apply for over 25% more jobs than men with the same skills and experience, to have the same number of call backs.

Name associated bias affects minority groups

This bias also exists for minority groups in places such as Australia, USA and UK.

Findings from an Australia National University Study demonstrated that to get as many interviews as a candidate with an Anglo-sounding name, an Indigenous candidate must submit 35% more applications, and a Chinese or Middle-Eastern person must submit over 60% more".

An easy fix

There are easy solutions to these biases, if we are prepared to make a simple change. For example, just by removing the name from the top of the resume when it's given to the hiring manager, can make a drastic difference to the opportunity for unconscious bias.

Perhaps historically, we needed the names at the top of the resume when applications were sent in the post. But now it's so easy to anonymise resumes, even if it's just for the initial screening. An HR Manager could remove the name before they send it on, and there are also tools available from companies like 'RemiPeople', which do all the anonymising for you. They even make the interview process fairer too.

Piano Police

At age 11 I was playing piano after school every day, and couldn't understand why anyone would want to stop learning to play, voluntarily. It transpired that nearly everyone I knew who ever played the piano, gave it up when they were about 12 years old. They all told me not to quit, citing it as one of their biggest regrets.

However, the system had other plans, and did its best to kill off any passion I had for playing. I was able to get to Grade 5 in 'Practical Piano' but to keep progressing, there were piano regulations I had to follow including passing 5 theory exams before I could continue. Although I could read music well, I had little interest in learning about 'time signatures, compositions and ornaments'. At 12 years old I didn't want to invest the months or years needed to pass the theory exams, and so decided to take a break. As is the case with many teens with other things to do, I never went back to it.

That was entirely my choice, but the system I was in played a role too. Rather than encourage 12 year olds to continue to play, they did the opposite. It was counter-productive to the industry that is in danger of fading out completely.

Who is going to challenge these rules, before it's too late? The old system had killed off my passion for piano, and I know I'm not the only one. I take full responsibility for my decision to stop, but the situation is indicative of a system that hasn't got it right when it comes to helping children embrace subjects that aren't academic, and only works for the few, not the many.

"Prepare students for their future not our past."
Ian Jukes

There are too many examples of people who have been discouraged from following their passion for creating new music, design, or other humanities and art subjects.

I was told by my computer studies teacher in 1988 that there was no future in computers and I shouldn't get into it. At the time, I thought it strange that someone who was given the responsibility of teaching computing, actually discouraged them from pursuing it. I couldn't help thinking that even if he was right and there was no future in the subject he was teaching, he was clearly in the wrong job and shouldn't be giving career advice. I ignored his comments, but I wondered how many acted on them.
How can we prepare the upcoming generations for jobs that haven't even been created yet; and for industries that haven't been discovered?

Paul McCartney went through his entire school life without his musical talent being noticed. George Harrison was in the same class as Paul and was missed too. Imagine a world without The Beatles!

We need to spend time identifying strengths and seeing where they appear, even if that's not in maths, languages or science. It is also up to us to know when to break the rules and believe in our judgement.

Teachers need to break school rules too

It's not the teachers' fault. The system is too focused on only considering academic indicators and imposing needless bureaucracy through an outdated curriculum.

So many brilliant teachers are constrained by an outdated system. They either have to break the rules, or create their own tools and systems. Then the teachers can play to their strengths and fulfil their potential, as well as the children's.

Fortunately, there are green shoots of progress with some schools beginning to change the approach to learning, but there's a long way to go.

Grouping classes by age has been an easy way to operate schools, and has served the needs of the Industrial Age, but there are other options more relevant to the needs of today.

An alternative method is to group children based on their ability and learning needs.

The zone of proximal development considers the difference between what a child can do with assistance, versus without any help. Soviet psychologist Lev Vygotsky recognised that children first learn by imitating adults. Initially, they are unable to successfully complete a task without assistance, but over time they are able to learn to complete it themselves. It's not just the result that's important, but the way they problem solve. Vygotsky believed that the role of a teaching system was to give children experiences that were within their zones of proximal development, and therefore develop their personal learning style and skills. Teachers should become the 'scaffolding' to support learning, rather than to instruct and command.

A few schools have embraced this concept and integrated it into the way their students are taught, including in some schools in Victoria, Australia. The teachers obtain a comprehensive understanding of each student's zone of proximal development which enables them to identify each student's next steps in learning. Unlike other schools, children are not grouped together just based on age. They're grouped using capability measures, and children will move zones based on their development, changing groups wherever the need arises.

It's not just the style of learning and teaching that's open; some schools decide to knock down walls to create additional flexibility, fluidity and openness. One school in particular states that *"the teachers plan and teach in teams to deliver an integrated approach to curriculum with a particular emphasis on ensuring strong skills in literacy and numeracy. In addition to the discipline based learning, students explore different ways of thinking, solving problems and communicating. They learn to use a range of technologies to plan, analyse, evaluate and present their work. Children learn about creativity, design principles and processes with a key focus on Communication, Thinking Curriculum, Design, Creativity and Information & Communication Technology."*

Lessons at Canterbury Primary (a government school) are also more fluid can change based on topics and questions raised by the children to help them learn in the best way possible. For example, the lesson may begin talking about the solar system, then a question could pop up from a child about black holes. Rather than ignoring a topic that may not have been part of the lesson plan, the teacher can Google black holes in real time, and begin exploring what comes up from that search. This shapes the next phase of the lesson and helps develop divergent thinking in the children. The Montessori school system is another alternative approach, that encourages independent learning, with the primary focus on the child's need, rather the need of a mass school system.

Clocks or Clouds?

Karl Popper was an Austro-British philosopher that made the observation that problems were either clocks or clouds. To fix a clock you can reverse engineer a solution by taking apart a similar clock, putting it back together and learning what makes it tick. It can therefore be fixed using deductive reasoning, a primary skill needed in the academic education system set up in 1870 to feed the labour need of the Industrial Revolution.

In contrast, a cloud cannot be reverse-engineered by simply looking at another cloud and breaking it into parts. You have to understand the whole weather system that created the cloud.

Business problems used to require workers to apply deductive reasoning to solve them and is a reason why the education system valued this skill. Nowadays, these clock problems can often be solved by computers and technology. The problems that most successful businesses now face in this increasingly complex world, are clouds.

To create the next big thing, or breakthrough idea, divergent thinking is going to be far more useful than deductive reasoning.

Organisations aren't machines

Organisations are treated like machines. Taylor's theory of scientific management, that Ford adopted to create the first assembly line, is based on improving economic efficiency and labour productivity. The command and control approach to management, which is also the approach often used at school, is how machines operate; by issuing a command you can control the output. Even organisational charts look like machine-charts or decision trees.

One of the rules that applies to improving machines has also been applied to people in organisations; to focus on their weaknesses. While it's a great way to improve the effectiveness of machines, as we've discussed, it's not the case for people. There's a far greater benefit in focusing on an individual's strengths, as it'll simultaneously increase productivity, performance and morale.

Taking a mechanistic approach to improvements may have worked previously, but now entire industries are changing fast, a creative approach is needed.

When people have historically been promoted and rewarded for doing what they are told, it can be a cultural shock when they're suddenly expected to come up with a new approach.

The race to the bottom allows you to treat your organisation like a machine. But now you need to win the race to the top with a culture and team that embraces creativity, flexibility, diversity, humanity, and that plays to their strengths.

The Meeting Epidemic

Meetings turned out to be a vital component of the Industrial Age. Being able to clearly communicate what tasks needed to be completed to hundreds of workers could only be done effectively by getting everyone together.

This habit never stopped, but now there's a meeting epidemic, even when far more effective communication methods are available.

Over time meetings have lost their focus, and have become a parasite to organisational creativity. What was once an integral component to the smooth running of a factory the meeting more often than not wastes time, and diffuses responsibility. The need to get 'buy-in' and feed the other managers' narcissistic need for inclusion creates the perfect storm for responsibility to simply disappear in a meeting. If you want to keep yourself in the clear if something goes wrong, it seems the best way is to share the idea at a meeting and then somehow it's not your fault because you told everyone about it.

Meetings are most dangerous when they're held to create the illusion of progress, and the appearance of action.

Al Pittampalli argues in his book, 'Modern Meeting Standard', that all meetings do is dilute quality ideas and reduce individual risk. It's not the only way, or even the best way, to communicate information or progress updates as it was 100 years ago. There are so many other alternatives to sharing information and making decisions, with tools like Asana, Trello or MS Teams. Document sharing with Google Drive or Sharepoint, has made it easy to keep one version that everyone can update at the same time, so you can have people in multiple locations contributing at a time that works for them.

How many times have you been invited to a meeting and realised very quickly you didn't need to be there?

"You must have a meeting to update everyone" is a good rule to consider breaking. There are more effective and efficient ways of sharing information and making decisions, if you are willing to think creatively and try something new.

Another habit that's good to break is allocating an hour. If you have back-to-back meetings, there's no time to get from one to the next, so you're either going to miss something or everyone else will waste time waiting for latecomers. It's just become a default to fit into calendar schedules. You can likely accomplish in 45 minutes, what you allocate an hour for. Try it out, you could recover an extra day every week with the time you save.

Living the dream

Another dynamic that enabled the success of the Industrial Revolution was the ability of marketing teams to stimulate desire for status. If someone did their job well, they would increase their status thanks to the new car or TV that they could now afford. Organisations and governments fuelled the dream of home-ownership, and happy to help people link success with status symbols. Not only did it help drive demand for products, it created a mechanic whereby the organisation could motivate staff by paying them more if they met their targets. Thanks to consumerism, there was a perceived status value as well as financial. You didn't have to tell people you were a success, your new car did that for you.

This system has the bonus, that measures of success and status are continually being raised, and are limitless. The new car you bought today, somehow doesn't seem so valuable when your neighbour drives up in an even better car the next day. Before you know it, you want another new car, and may be prepared to sacrifice a little more of who you are to get it.

For hundreds of years, people have been promised that if they do what they're told, work hard and remain loyal then they will be rewarded with a safe and stable job that will give them status. While this may have been guaranteed in the past, it isn't possible today, and as a result people can feel disappointed, betrayed and angry.

Roles can change overnight, entire industries are shifting, and it's happening quicker than ever before. The warning signs have been around for years but many haven't taken notice. Your industry is being disrupted; the trouble is that most businesses leave it far too late before they start to change. The corporate landscape is littered with businesses that didn't just wonder 'who moved my cheese', but instead were shocked that their entire block of cheese had disappeared forever. This is not a small shift in strategy; this is a fundamental change to the whole system.

Since your first day at school when you were told to put your hand up if you wanted to be heard, you've waited to be chosen, to answer a question or to be picked for a team. No-one tells you when this needs to change, and if you keep waiting to be picked now, and be told what to do, you could be waiting a very, very long time.

Now is the best opportunity you've had to cement your security and make a real difference. But don't wait for your boss to start it for you. You need to pick yourself.

Be the best in the world

In an economy where scarcity is valuable, it pays to be the best. You just need to choose what you want to be best at, and what you want your 'world' to be. Being the best in the world doesn't
mean you have to be number 1 out of 7 billion people. You can define what your world is. Maybe it's the best barista in your town, or the fastest mobile phone repairer. Perhaps you could do something that even the largest companies don't do, like John Papandriopoulos who was the first to turn his iPhone into a full action camera, that took 20 high quality photos in a second, with his SnappyCam app.

Video didn't kill the radio star

During the 2000s the music industry was very publicly dragged kicking and screaming into a new technological era, fighting the change every step of the way. Instead of embracing the opportunities that came with file sharing, and then streaming, the bigwigs of the music industry administered the same tactics that had kept them in their jobs for decades. It failed disastrously.

Technological change was not new to the music industry. Vinyl LP records gave music a new way of providing the listener control over what they heard. But its introduction didn't stop people listening to the radio, as some had feared it would. Nor did it when the audio cassette tape was invented by Philips in 1962. It increased the interest of popular music on the radio, and created new revenue opportunities.

Video was apparently going to kill the radio star when MTV launched in 1981, but it didn't. It again gave music another marketing channel and changed the way music was appreciated. It opened up possibilities for artists, record companies and fans alike. The success was also in part due to the technological advancements of the affordable video player, as well as the progress that had been made in the studio.

The same year that MTV launched, also saw the introduction of the Compact Disc and in October 1981 the first CD Album, Billy Joel's 52nd Street, was released along with Sony's CD player. It began one of the most profitable periods for record companies, who had costs of only 75 cents per CD in the mid 1980s, and enjoyed a mark-up of over 2,000%. The customer received a perceived improvement to their musical experience, and paid extra for it.

So why then did the music industry fail so severely during the emergence of file sharing? One of the key reasons was they failed the people that had made them so successful, their customers. Amazingly, they didn't just stop listening to them, they went up against them legally. Rather than bringing their biggest supporters along with them, in 1991 they took the file sharing site Napster to court, along with threatening legal action against thousands of its users.

The profits that the music industry had enjoyed for decades were suddenly under threat, and the industry panicked. Rather than work with their customers, they tried to force them to comply, and the result was a disaster.

Soon, the same customers the music industry had come to depend on, deserted them, and took to digital music. Almost overnight, Apple's iTunes became the number 1 music distributor. You could instantly get virtually any music track, from any genre, on your music player. The number of people listening to music increased, and there are still billions of dollars being made in the industry, just not by the same bigwigs as before. It's not enough to just react to change any more; by the time you've done that it's time to change again. You have to lead the change, but the problem is that the rules we learnt at school don't apply any more. We need a new rulebook.

"If you do what you always did, you'll get what you always got."

Not even that holds any more.

This saying was originally meant to motivate people to change, but as if you did what you always did, you'd just get what you always got. Even that fall-back isn't a guarantee any more.

If you don't change your products, services, approach, attitudes to take advantage of the changing world, you'll get left behind. How many people's budgets are prepared by first copying what happened in the previous year, and then tweaking a few numbers for the next 12 months? How many brand plans are a copy and paste of what was done last year? Sure, there may be an exciting relaunch in fancy new packaging, or maybe even a new flavour toothpaste, or cars with automated reverse parking as standard.

But what are you doing to re-shape the market, and connect with your customers to find out what they really want?

It would be nice if you could guarantee the same results tomorrow by doing what you did yesterday. But you can't.

Previously, in a world where mass marketing and sales appealed to a wide group of people, all you had to do was be the loudest. You could get away with the rinse and repeat approach and be paid very well for it. But now change happens fast, and lots of segments have been replaced by mass.

The phrase should now be 'If you always do what you always did, you may get a slice of what you always got, but don't count on it'. Not as catchy, but you get the point.

Stop Conforming!

We're continually telling children that they need to do what they are told throughout their education, to comply and conform. Then we're surprised when they're unable to get a job, because the hiring manager is looking for someone with creativity, and an ability to come up with new solutions to complex problems.

It's helpful to give people boundaries for them to push. Ironically the child with no limits, because their parents want them to be 'free-spirited', can end up anxious, clingy and insecure. Another child, with clear boundaries, and the freedom to challenge them, can find it much easier to embrace change and ambiguity.

It's this 'challenging' behaviour that isn't often taught in schools, because it can be mistaken for dissent, rather than being seen as a constructive growth of an idea. Most children spend the first 15 years of life being rewarded for doing what they are told, and being reprimanded for challenging authority or the status quo. Of course, there are rules that children need to follow so they can safely cross a road or avoid getting attacked by dogs, but too much compliance can also be a bad thing.
So managers shouldn't be surprised, when their staff find it hard to come up with original ideas, or they themselves don't see the tsunami of change approaching their industry.

Choose yourself

We are conditioned at school to get acknowledgment, or even permission, from a teacher to tell us we're good enough before we can proceed. If you're setting up your own business, trying to get on the best projects at work, looking for a job, or trying to get promoted, you can't just wait for permission.

Seth Godin has articulated in many different ways the

need to 'pick yourself'. In the old world, you could work hard and wait patiently to get that promotion. Those days are gone. Now it's up to you to take the initiative, and you need to get noticed.

You can't expect the people around you to help you get chosen, not even your manager – whether you deserve it or not. It's time to stand up, choose yourself and use the skills you have in a way that is going to add value.

Don't hold out for someone to tell you that you're ready, that you're good enough. Work out what 'good enough' looks like, and then make sure you know when you get there that you are ready to proceed. It's time to back yourself.

Steve Jobs was famous for backing himself, though that's not to say that he always made the best decisions first. On one day he would argue a point vigorously, and then after contemplation, would take the opposite viewpoint and argue it just as vociferously. His conviction was what made him a strong leader, he was often so passionate about his point, despite having argued the opposite the day before, that people didn't even see the change, and were captivated with the plan of today.

Jobs' successor, Apple CEO Tim Cook, sees this flip-flopping as a strength of the Apple mastermind. "I saw it daily. This is a gift, because things do change, and it takes courage to change. It takes courage to say, I was wrong". It's far more useful than a CEO that makes no decisions, or a team that always leave the hard decisions to someone else.

Closed for Busyness

How are you today? The most common response to this question in a work environment is 'I'm busy'. We live in a society that often values busyness over business. The belief that being busy is what matters comes from the

Industrial Revolution's factory approach to work. The busier you were, the more successful your business was. While this may be the case in some organisations today, it's certainly not causal. Just because you're busy, doesn't mean that you're successful, or even doing your job.

According to Laura Vanderkam from Fast Company, the ultimate definition of success is having a million things to do, and only doing a few of them.

Several years ago, I created Finish@4, a national campaign to encourage people to finish work at 4pm on 4 October. It was great to see people sign up for what I thought would be a relatively easy commitment, but in reality it unearthed some interesting stories through my discussions with CEOs. When questioned, many of the business leaders said that they found it hard to go home early because they felt guilty leaving before their staff. I also met with individuals within those companies to ask them why they worked so late. Interestingly, they didn't want to leave before the boss in case they were considered to have a poor work ethic.

So, the boss didn't want to go in case they looked lazy, and the staff wouldn't leave before the boss for the same reason.

This catch-22 could be solved if the leadership team went home on time.
Hard work is a critical ingredient for success, but it's not synonymous with continually working long hours. It doesn't even make sense from Fordism's perspective, where the most efficient were rewarded. Shouldn't we be recognising the account manager that can do their job in half the time, rather than person who takes 3 hours longer every day to do the same tasks?

Jody Thompson and Cali Ressler are two HR professionals that created a strategy for paying employees based on results rather than just for turning up from 9-5. It took significant effort and strategic influencing to encourage their organisation, Best Buy, to adopt their idea, but they did.

The results were so successful that their concept of a Results Only Work Environment (ROWE) has now been used many others.

In today's digital world, people can work from different locations, there's no need for them to be in an office all the time. There are too many managers whose primary reason their staff need to be in the office, is because they think 'working from home' means they're at the beach. This is a classic leadership trait of the controller who supervises rather than leads. If you trust your staff and give them the opportunity to themselves be trusted, you're likely to find that they can do the work without you looking over their shoulder.

With faster internet, cloud computing and increased security, there is no excuse for expecting people to be at work all day every day. It's inefficient as you have to pay for their office space 24-7. Global banks, tech companies and media organisations have moved to an activity-based working environment where you don't have your own desk. Surveys showed that staff were only at their permanent workspaces for 50% of the time. Instead, there are 'home zones' where teams are based, but you're not assigned a specific desk and you can just as easily work in the on-site café or library. When managers focus on delivery measures not hours worked, and trust is encouraged rather than motivation based on fear, we see a cultural change that enables people to be rewarded for their contribution of value, not working unnecessary hours.

Workplace flexibility will be a defining measure of the successful businesses of the future. In the same way that those organisations who embraced technology in the early 2000s, are the only ones around today, I believe those organisations who embrace flexible working are likely to be the only ones around in 10-15 years.

Now is the time that you can stand out based on your merits, not for a virtual badge of honour for staying longer at the office. We need to show that there is more benefit playing to our strengths, delivering outstanding results and finishing our work on time. You have the opportunity to shine, to be great, to be part of the new future that doesn't value compliance, as much as it values people that can create value.

Give them their leaving speech today

Leaving speeches range from a quick thank you and a Danish pastry, to a tear-jerking talk where the manager reminisces of great times, achievements and career highlights.

The irony of this situation is worthy of its own celebration. How many resignations could have been avoided, if the individual's contribution had been recognised when they were in their role, rather than on their last day when it was all too late? Maybe they wouldn't have left at all.

The trouble is that it's not easy for every manager to open up and tell their staff how valuable they are. Usually the lack of appreciation is either linked to a concern that it will create an awkward situation, or people just don't make the time. Even worse, is the misplaced fear that their staff member will turn up to work the next day and use this new insight to negotiate a pay rise or a promotion.

In reality, if your staff are appreciated and can play to their strengths, they will perform better, productivity will increase, and you'll be the one getting the pay rise and promotion.

The Paradox of Work: The best way to stay safe is to avoid playing it safe

For years, hard work and compliance have been rewarded with a stable job, a secure future, healthcare and a retirement fund. But now, that model is broken, and there is no guaranteed future; there are no safe jobs. There used to be careers considered bulletproof, including finance, manufacturing and government. Even during restructures, it was likely that you would be relocated somewhere else within the organisation, rather than being removed. If you looked after the system, the system would look after you. Good, honest, compliant, hard-working individuals were looked after because they were what the system needed. For over 150 years it worked, production became cheaper, markets were created, people were given the security of a consistent wage, and thanks to the drive of consumerism, there was an increasing demand for producing quality products.

Then the world changed. We now live in a time where doing what you're told and working hard, isn't guaranteed to get you what you think you deserve.

Paradoxically, playing it safe is not the safe option, as Seth Godin also argues in the Icarus Deception. The race to the bottom is not a race worth winning, and it's unlikely that you'll win it.

The good news is that you can choose yourself. If you have a skill, a talent, an art, a craft, then the world needs you to make the most of it.

It comes as a surprise to some people, but it's not the role of your manager to make you money, and your organisation wasn't created to give you a job. The days are gone where you can simply work hard and wait to be promoted. If your role can be written down as a series of steps, then it could one day be replaced by a robot.

Your company may call itself a 'people focused

organisation' but ultimately, if they are involved in a race to the bottom, then cost will become the dominant driver of decisions. It's more important than ever that you know your strengths and how to utilise and market them.

If you want to move up the ladder, you need to choose yourself and make sure you, and the decision-makers know what you have to offer. Or build your own ladder. If you don't like the look of any jobs in your organisation, or others don't look like moving out any time soon, consider creating a new role. Identify what's most important to the organisation, that aligns with your strengths, and start to build your case. I've created multiple positions in my career using this idea, and there are many benefits. As the roles are based on your strengths, you will have a strong case when it comes to applying for it. You'll also be more likely to be successful in it.

Secondly, by showing the initiative for why the organisation would benefit from this new role, you'll already be adding another strength to your application, and be a front runner with others playing catch up.

It used to just be about doing. Now it's about creating. Creating value, creating something new, creating something different, shorter, sharper, longer, smoother, more efficient, greener. We live in a world of rapid change, where compliance has been replaced by those creating new possibilities, options and opportunities.

The world needs you to be you; and it needs you now.

Or as Hillel the Elder would have put it;

"If not you, who? If not now, when?"

PART 3

WHAT NEXT?

If you're keen to be part of the Strengths Revolution, there are some key changes you can take advantage of. They will help you determine which rules to break and how to play to your strengths in the new world:

Moving from Compliance to Trust.

It's not enough to get people to comply any more. School taught us that compliance was a useful tool, and rewarded us for it. But what we need now is to be able to trust ourselves and each other. We are entering a new era of workplace flexibility. If you need your staff to be sitting in front of you to know that they are delivering in their role, then what happens when you're not there? Trust them, give them the tools to perform, be clear with what is needed and support them. Trust is easier than compliance, not initially, but in the long term and by a long way.

What can you do differently to trust your team more, trust your customers and to trust yourself?

From Instruction to Curiosity

You need your team to be curious if you want them to come up with new ideas, create better processes and identify new opportunities to help you stay ahead of the game. Curiosity is squeezed out of us as we grow up. I've heard too many adults telling small children to stop asking so many questions, presumably because it's annoying them having to respond.

It happens at work too, although often more subtly. We tell people what to do because it's easy. But if you want people to be creative, you need the right environment, culture and conditions. You can't just tell them to innovate. I was a junior in a management consultancy many years ago, when the General Manager of a client who wanted his company to be more creative, said to us in front of his executive team: "Tell us what to innovate and we'll innovate it'. At first I thought he was being ironic, as by every other indicator he was an outstanding and strategic leader, but unfortunately, he wasn't joking. He was conditioned into being instructed, and instructing, and had no concept of how debilitating the environment had become. Innovation isn't a button that you can just press, or just carried out by one role in the organisation. It's a way of thinking, and depends on the right environment and attitude for teams to be creative and make decisions.

Curiosity was always a part of who you were. The school or work system may have stripped it out of you, or just not valued it, but we need you to be curious now.

We need to support people with opportunities to be creative, encourage ideas and an environment where people can have a go, even if it doesn't go to plan. If it doesn't work, they can learn from it and try again. Let them 'newton' as much as they can, with enough time and space to be curious; who knows who's on the verge of the next iPhone?

From Conformity to Diversity

The Industrial Age needed conformity. It required replaceable cogs in a big machine that could be changed whenever required, literally and metaphorically. This system didn't support diversity, so it was removed at every opportunity.

The trouble now is, any job that can be broken down into a series of processes can be replaced by AI one day. The previously safe areas such as finance, sales and retail have already been disrupted significantly, and will be again.

Even some successful lawyers who've studied for years have had their roles been replaced. You can put a legally binding will together on my-will-online.com.au or even get divorced on OnlineDivorce.com

We still need academic skills and people that have expertise in law, finance and medicine, but the system shouldn't be stopping diversity, it needs to encourage it.

Managers often hire people similar to themselves, because they feel like a 'good fit'. If you need a team to come up with new ideas, or better processes, select diverse people.

This Affinity Bias has more dangerous implications than just creating teams that aren't as creative or dynamic as they need to be. Affinity bias is often unconscious and results in managers hiring people like themselves, which isn't a fair way of recruiting. In many engineering and tech fields, where there is already a bias in gender and ethnicity, affinity bias will accentuate the problem and increase the likelihood, for example, that the males will recruit more males. It's often unconscious bias, and the impacts are real and need addressing, more now than ever before.

There are solutions to removing bias that are extremely simple.

Screens in orchestra auditions removed bias, and the same impact is possible using anonymous resumes and other screening tools.

If you want to see change happen, the solutions are here already. The world is waiting for people like you to take a stand and make it happen. It's not the technology that's holding us back; it's inertia and apathy. Be the change you want to see.

Do it today. Do it now.

From Machinery to Humanity

As a result of Fordism, we've been organising people like they are replaceable cogs in a machine.

If I want to make a shoe polishing machine more efficient, I can give it a tune-up or upgrade parts; but it won't come up with innovative ways of polishing shoes. It can't create the idea to donate a free pair of shoes to an impoverished child, with every shoe sale, like Tomshoes.com. The value of an organisation is its people, and we need to embrace this more than ever before.

Treating the organisation as a machine doesn't work. If you want to stay ahead in the new world, you need to show your people empathy, and enable them to play to their strengths in an environment they can 'newton'.

Bringing more humanity benefits everyone. Steven Covey gives an excellent example of the importance of empathy, when he describes a situation with two children on a busy train. They're running up and down the carriage, making noise and annoying the morning commuters on their way to work. Passengers raised their eyebrows and were increasingly irritated. The dad did doing nothing, so finally one of the businessmen who'd had enough asks him to keep his children quiet. The father replies: "Sorry, I was in a world of my own; we're on our way back from the hospital where their mother has just died. I'll tell them to keep it down".

Empathy plays an increasingly important role in the human world, which wasn't useful during the Industrial Age. Being able to see things from another person's perspective not only helps us to expand our mind, it shows that we are actively listening to them. Instead of creating conflict or confusion, we can help reach new solutions. If your organisation has customers, it's more important than ever before to understand and meet their needs, so where better to start than empathy?

From Consistency to Creativity

In an industrial economy, consistency wins. Producing the same thing over and over again with exactly the same outcome is what made Ford successful. Today creativity is what's needed to come up with ways to add value that people will pay for, contribute to or engage with.

You are creative, you may just not know how, or need to unlearn or relearn. There are many ways to be creative, but you need to allow yourself and others the space to try new things and fail along the way. Often we don't try to be creative because we feel we need to come up with an excellent result.

Sometimes it's a fear of being ridiculed that goes right back to being at school or a need for perfection. Often we put high expectations on ourselves, which can ultimately stop us trying out different skills, approaches or ideas.

Being more creative is another path you can start on today.

Choose your rocks

The following story was told to me by Amanda Tilley, an inspiring leader who always gave her managers the freedom to play to their strengths:

A teacher enters the classroom with a large glass jar. She places large rocks in it until there isn't any more room.

"Is it full?" she asks the students. They agree that it's full.

Then she takes out a bag of gravel, which she pours into the jar. "Now is it full?" They agree that it's now full. She then takes out a bag of sand, which she pours into the jar. "Is it full now?" she asks. With a little hesitation and a few wry smiles, they agree that now, at last, it's full.

She finally takes out a jug of water, which she pours into the jar until it spills over.
"Ok, now it's full."

"So what's the lesson?" she asks her class.

One of the students answers: "There's always room for more?"

"A good answer, but it's even more than that." the teacher replies. "It's that you have to ensure you prioritise the most important aspects of your life. If I had put the water, sand and gravel in first, there wouldn't have been enough room for the big rocks".

The moral of the story applies perfectly when considering the art of playing to your strengths. You have to be aware of what your strengths are and make room for them. If you don't make time to focus on developing your strengths, there are plenty of other demands in your life that will happily force their way in.

Apple CEO Tim Cook learnt the value of focusing on strengths from his predecessor Steve Jobs: "Focus is key. Not just in running a company, but your personal life, as well. You can only do so many things great, cast aside everything else."

If you feel that you have no strengths, speak to friends, family or colleagues to find out what strengths they see in you. You may want to try something new which could unearth your hidden talents. Clifton Strengths Finder from Gallup is a useful tool to begin with, or the VIA Assessment.

It doesn't hurt to remind yourself, that you can be whoever you want, and not who others want you to be. In any moment you can change your mind, your ideas, your views, the way you treat people, whether you say yes, how often you say no, who you help, who you are friends with. Change happens in an instant. Convincing ourselves of the need to change is what takes the time, if we let it.

The Industrial Revolution needed you to be the right person for their factories, so they created a school system to shape you that way. Not only is that not useful today, but it's also holding you back.

You don't need to be good at everything, this is a time where you can, and need to, play to your strengths.

It's up to you.

So don't just put your hand up, stand up.

Don't feel you need to be good at everything.

Pick something and become great at it.

Back yourself.

Play to your strengths.

Now.

ACKNOWLEDGEMENTS

A very special thanks to Simon McMac for helping me with research for this book, with conversation as diverse as the Age of Enlightenment to the Japanese translation of words that don't even exist. Your dedication to tackling life-changing challenges head on will forever be an inspiration. I will never forget you and your spirit lives on forever.

Love and thanks to Rhian for your support, thoughts and passion. You're my rock and my light – to have someone with me on this crazy ride that is different every day is something that I will never take for granted. The world needs more people like you :)

A big thank you to Mum for raising me to play to my strengths from day one, and sacrificing so much to give me so many opportunities.

Laura, your wit is unparalleled, and your ability to make anyone laugh in any situation is fantastic. Your approach to beating the system that tried to cage your ballet creativity was world-class too. Who'd have thought that passing out just before your exam would have made the papers? APSNDx.

Thanks to Seth Godin, the most influential marketing mind in the world & despite being followed by millions always responds to my emails the same day. If you want to know what remarkable is, read Purple Cow.

Thanks to Mike Stewart, my mentor, who changed the world and had his own rule book. You and Robyn defined greatness and were the original 'Notebook' couple; it was such a shame that your final chapter had to end the same way.

Thanks to Amanda for taking a risk and hiring me even though I was left-field and not the safe option. A more passionate person you won't find, and someone who understands which little things are really the big things.

Finally, thanks to Zara, Lea and Maxwell. Your fearlessness in a child's world where everything changes every day, is something I continually learn from and will always be inspired by.

If you've found this book useful, please consider spreading the word to help more people play to their strengths. Perhaps buy a book for each of your team, start a thread on LinkedIn, post on Facebook, or lend this copy to someone you think would appreciate it.

Breaking Good.